STRANGE PARADISE
Portrait of a Marriage

BOOKS BY GRACE SCHULMAN

POETRY

Without a Claim
The Broken String
Days of Wonder: New and Selected Poems
The Paintings of Our Lives
For That Day Only
Hemispheres
Burn Down the Icons

TRANSLATION

Songs of Cifar: Poems (with Ann McCarthy de Zavala)
by Pablo Antonio Cuadra
At the Stone of Losses: Poems by T. Carmi

CRITICISM AND ESSAYS

Marianne Moore: The Poetry of Engagement
First Loves and Other Adventures

EDITION

The Poems of Marianne Moore (Authorized Edition)

MEMOIR

Strange Paradise: Portrait of a Marriage

GRACE SCHULMAN

STRANGE PARADISE
Portrait of a Marriage

Turtle Point Press
Brooklyn, New York

Requests for permission to make copies of any
part of the work should be sent to:
Turtle Point Press
info@turtlepointpress.com

Library of Congress Cataloging-in-Publication Data
is available from the publisher upon request

Design by Cooley Design Lab

ISBN: 978-1-885983-52-7
Ebook ISBN: 978-1-885983-62-6

Printed in the United States of America

Jerome L. Schulman, 1927–2016

*"that strange paradise
unlike flesh, gold, or stately buildings,
the choicest piece of my life:
the heart rising
in its estate of peace"*

Marianne Moore, "Marriage"

Marriage is the highest mystery.

Novalis

CONTENTS

1

THE FOUNTAIN

When Alan Gilbert raised his baton at Avery Fisher Hall on November 30, 2013, I slid forward in my seat. Mozart's Symphony No. 41, the "Jupiter." We'd heard it before, Jerry and I, in our fifty-four-year marriage, but each time it told us something new. During the intermission, Jerry spoke of the percussion rumblings, the silvery harmonics, the magic. "It was the fire of his last years," he said, having read that it was composed only three years before Mozart's death. When the concert was over, I stood with the crowd for an ovation. Jerry couldn't stand. Sidestepping out of our row, I retrieved his folding wheelchair to push him up the aisle, and we waited downstairs for a hired car that would take us home. I knew he was in pain.

Ironically, it was his long, fast stride that I remembered from when we first met, in Washington Square Park. I hadn't expected to go to there that Sunday, wanting instead to stay in and get to know the studio apartment I had just rented, for eighty dollars a month plus electric, in a gangly twenty-two-story brick building on University Place, in Greenwich Village. I left my new home only when one of the maintenance workers who'd helped me move chairs in, a burly man from Jamaica given to humming fragments of gospel songs, said I needed air. That day, noticing my guitar balanced precariously on top of a stack of china cups, he directed me to the park, diagonally across the street from my building, where, he said, slowly and with emphasis, "You can play in the fountain."

I was astonished. What he called the fountain was a limestone circle in the center of the park which, when dry, was brimming with another kind of energy. Faces, crowds of animated faces, people, like me, in their mid-twenties, were singing out "Wimoweh" and "Suliram" and "Down by the Riverside" (with its refrain, "Study war no more"), as though their fervor alone could achieve peace on earth. Nineteen fifty-seven was a year of innocent hope, and these believers rallied, unaware that their dreams would be dashed in the following decade.

In the pre-beatnik fifties, folksingers John Jacob Niles and Susan Reed were the progenitors of Bob Dylan and the Beatles. Alan Lomax and his father, John, hunted work songs and prison chants in America, then collected ballads abroad. Their followers, the fountain singers, were wearing torn jeans and plaid shirts, their Sunday-in-the-park clothes, although I'd seen one of the men that Friday dressed in tweeds for his job.

Sometimes the singers performed individually. A woman on the far ledge offered a bluegrass song from her native Kentucky, accompanied by, she announced, a dulcimer plucked with a turkey quill. Her abiding influence was Jean Ritchie, who gathered Appalachian songs and popularized the dulcimer. Playing an English sea chantey on a guitar was a man I recognized from a news photo as Israel (Izzy) Young, who ran the Folklore Center on nearby MacDougal Street. Izzy was an activist whose only cause was fighting the frequent neighborhood bans on outdoor music. I spoke with him long enough to learn that the actor Theodore Bikel often tried out Austrian ballads here, even before he performed Rodgers and Hammerstein's "Edelweiss" in *The Sound of Music* on Broadway.

In that stone ambiance on a cool September late afternoon, I sat strumming the guitar my father had bought for me while I was a student at Bard College five years before. Raised on West Eighty-Sixth Street in Manhattan, I was singing a rural Scotch-Irish ballad whose origin was far from mine. It began, "She was a lass from the low country." I was trying not to look at the man with cropped auburn hair who was sitting on the fountain rim next to me and did not sing. He seemed a few years older than the musicians around him, but he had a boy's gaze and a youthful way of waving his long arms. I was drawn to his hazel eyes, alert, then darting, which shone when his smile made creases at their corners. Because he did not meet my eyes, I thought he was listening to others, not to me. I was wrong.

We didn't speak. "Venga Jaleo," "Röslein," and "Greensleeves" went by, our glances still wandering around or beyond each other. I had been informed that it was illegal to sing after six o'clock, and invited some twenty folksingers to my apartment across the Square. A guitarist who enunciated Romanian lullabies thought that the man with cropped auburn hair and hazel eyes was with a pretty young woman nearby, and, with my permission, asked the man to join us. The man wasn't with anyone.

Back at my place, "Michael, Row," a spiritual, started up, to the dismay of neighbors objecting to noise. Still the man was silent. (I didn't know at the time that his behavior was characteristic: he would say, years later, "Silence is the supreme contribution to conversation.") That night he left early, having surreptitiously copied the number on my telephone. He dialed it within an hour, announced his name, Jerry Schulman, and said in a low, unassuming voice that friends had left him theater tickets to *West Side Story* the next evening and would I join him. When I accepted he asked me to be ready at six and said we'd travel uptown together. The lie was transparent—though charming: the next night was a Monday, with its interval between performances, and his offer was a ruse to see me. It worked. Jerry appeared at the prearranged time and apologized for the change in plan.

"The theater is closed tonight, and I don't have friends who leave me tickets. I just wanted to see you."

Disarming. I played the show's score on a record player. The song we liked best was "One Hand, One Heart," a marriage vow based on a traditional Spanish hymn to God. As the last notes faded we looked at each other directly, unsmiling.

I was attracted but not smitten. Not yet. My bliss was walking unencumbered through the winding streets west of the park, so much more inviting than the rigid rectangles in the uptown neighborhood of my childhood. I was intent on a career as a news reporter, hard for a woman to manage in the 1950s. Then, too, a very early relationship with an older man, a C.I.A. operative, in Washington, D.C., had soured me on romance. When he pressed me to sublimate my ambition to his furtive career, I left that spy. The cage unlocked, the door opened, and I saw the world anew.

Alone at last, I was bound for an enlightened single life. If romance had to be followed by marriage—a common precept in those years—I'd have none of it. Still, I was drawn to this new acquaintance from the fountain. I was taken by his eyes, which had the intense gaze of an El Greco saint, and his voice, which was low-pitched and smooth with a ragged edge, the pauses between phrases indicating that he was examining a subject from all sides.

As we talked that night, my interest grew.

"Did you enjoy the folk singing yesterday?" Jerry asked.

"Yes."

"I treasured it."

Not knowing how to respond, I picked up the guitar, tuned it, and played an old French song, "À la claire fontaine." In it, a woman bathing in a fountain by moonlight remembers her lost love and regrets deeds undone. As I sang I thought, Why bathe in a fountain? As with other ballads, the details are exact—three ravens, four horses—but the central situation is a mystery. I slowed down on the refrain:

> Il ya longtemps que je t'aime
> jamais je ne t'oublierais.

Jerry spoke, swaying to the music: "That's how I feel."

"About a lost love??"

"No, about the fountain."

I doubted Jerry's enthusiasm, but only at first. I saw him

listen to Carol Lawrence and Larry Kert singing on the record we played of *West Side Story*. I heard him speak of Mozart, whose symphonies he had first heard live in Salzburg in 1954. At the time, he was an Army captain medical doctor with a field artillery battalion stationed in Germany. He had gone with a fellow officer who did not love the music as he did. When I told him I'd just recovered from Asian flu, he said that he was a physician doing research in influenza virus. Noting his modest expertise, I assumed he was good at his profession.

His presence was sparkling, and yet we hardly knew each other. He was open to the arts, especially, I thought, for a physician, but his receptiveness could be simply the momentary appeal of a woman playing the guitar, withdrawn the next day. What if his mind were closed, his views unacceptable? What if we were hopelessly at odds? I was to express those doubts to him on a subsequent meeting when he would reply "Inconceivable" and go on stroking my shoulder. From early on, he had a way of thinking me better than I was, less difficult, less mercurial. I wanted to become the woman he had in mind.

On that first night, we ordered a moussaka delivery from a nearby restaurant and placed the plastic boxes on a table made from a door I'd sanded down and varnished. Unfortunately, the brass legs, badly attached, buckled under. With apologies, I brought a tray to my huge bed, and we settled there.

Yes, we spent that night in the apartment building we were to live in, that he was to die in.

The recognition that we were in love came early. After a five-dollar dinner for two—Jerry's treat—at Rocco's on Sullivan

Street, we walked home through the park, where white-to-purple hydrangeas glowed even in the dark. We reached my apartment singing "I Could Write a Book," off-key but in tune with each other. In the park an elm screened a full moon, close to the earth and with a blue-gold halo in humid air. I looked up at the elm, and at him, which was a pleasure: I was unusually tall, standing shoeless at six feet, and he topped that at six feet two. He proposed marriage a week after we met. I held back for two years. I wanted first to find work on a New York paper, and I knew that to most city editors, married women were anathema.

In the meantime, we went to the Metropolitan Opera and heard *La Bohème* from the fourth tier. It felt odd initially to see Jerry weep for Colline, who sings a bass farewell to the overcoat he has to sell. Finally, though, I was moved. At my place, we put on a long-playing record and danced soft-shoe incongruously to Beethoven's Seventh Symphony. Walking down the street for dinner, we stood before the house where Henry James set his novel *Washington Square*, bought a paperback, went back, and read scenes aloud to one another. Jerry picked out the phrase "luminous vagueness" in the description of Dr. Sloper, and, seeing me smile, repeated it.

"Is this the house where Henry James's grandmother lived?" he asked.

"Yes, I think so."

"It's supposed to have marble steps and to have very quiet neighbors. It's not the same," he said, looking at the book.

"Things change," I offered.

"We never will."

"We ought to celebrate our love with presents," Jerry said that first year. On Eighth Street we bought a long-playing record album for me and for him a pipe whose white bowl resembled a soap castle. We ate paella in a restaurant on MacDougal Street and wrote down the ingredients so we could cook it at home.

Shortly after we met, Jerry bought a guitar at Izzy's Center, and we played songs of Huddie Ledbetter ("Lead Belly"), which we picked up from a book edited by Alan Lomax. In Jerry's top-down Austin-Healey, our long legs entangled somewhere under the hood, we drove to the Newport Folk Festival. There, on the Rhode Island seashore, we slept in a tent on the beach, walked barefoot in the oncoming tide, and, sitting on the grass at Fort Adams State Park, heard a slender woman sing "Virgin Mary Had a Little Baby," a woman who later sang to the world as Joan Baez. "I went to college nearby, but it was never like this. I missed the tones," he said. Music accompanied our early encounters, and it never faded.

My street lay between two muddy rivers, rust-red at sunset. We liked to walk from the East River, really an inlet, to the Hudson, where we'd look out at New Jersey. Once the Hudson's wharves held commercial steamers; now one was a depot for errant cars and another a dry dock for an aircraft carrier. Nearest my apartment was the Gansevoort pier, a bare landing that was to become a park for writers and for families with baby strollers. Shortly after sunrise, the waters were murky green, but in places they glistened as though reborn. Ailanthus trees shimmered with gleaming questions. On the way to the river, we'd glanced upward to see the lofty, tawny-red towers of downtown buildings that seemed to be following us. I remarked on the illusion, while Jerry was at pains to discover just why we saw them that way. Avenues were ghosted with fog that lifted as we spoke. This was our river, our neighborhood, our city.

What intrigued me about Jerry was his relentlessly inquisitive mind. I had never known anyone with his irreverence for received knowledge. Jerry challenged easy truths, as I discovered early on. He probed established formulas. Take the morning after a lightning storm, when we ventured outside. Suddenly he breathed deep and tasted the air. "Can you smell the ozone?" he asked.

"I know it's there."

"Yes, but can you *smell* it? It's supposed to follow lightning, but how can we be sure?"

Or the night we'd come home from a concert at Carnegie Hall to my place. It was late, the traffic was raucous, and we were glad to relax in one big room containing the immense bed and the still-unsteady table that held my typewriter and our meals. While I tinkered with a stovetop espresso maker he had bought for us on Bleecker Street, I noticed Jerry grow distant, forcing his attempts at conversation. He courted me as usual, and we made love with no lessening of ardor. But later that night I woke to see a coin spinning to catch the light from the table lamp. Jerry sat at the homemade table in his pajamas, tossing a penny high in the air. Was he trying to decide something? I wondered. No, his coin toss was to question one of the laws of probability. Four hours, four hundred heads, only forty tails, he said next morning. Not even the final toss—at 6 a.m.—could slake his hunger.

He carried an air of mystery. He was alive with opposites: easy in manner yet stern about principles; a languid walker yet quick in an emergency; casual and yet traditional. In the process of questioning things, from the wind's direction when he'd run with a kite to the premises of natural laws, he surprised me constantly. Following each of his changes was, for me, like entering a wrought-iron door opening to another door opening to a dark stairway, as in the narrow houses on our side streets. I knew his background, his predilections for Dickens and Mahler, his long arm that reached for a glass of gift Yquem, his slim torso in the cotton T-shirts I bought for him. And yet I didn't know him at all.

In a generation that eschewed living together before marriage, Jerry and I usually slept in my apartment on the Square. On Sundays, we were careful to avoid my father, who would silently leave bagels and Danish outside my door. There was a duality in his understanding, not uncommon in the fifties. He assumed we made love while simultaneously expecting that his unmarried daughter was chaste. He never spoke of it.

On one of his visits I opened the door, unthinking, and Jerry rapidly blurted, "I came over to drive her to the Grand Army Plaza Library in Brooklyn, open on Sundays." My father glimpsed the unmarried lovers, left the packages, and disappeared. Jerry confessed, "I know he didn't believe me. But he liked that I offered him a proper excuse for being there."

Jerry kept a sunny, white-walled apartment he rented before we met, a walkup in the East Sixties, close to his lab at Cornell Medical College. Even at the height of our joys, I secretly wished for free hours alone. The adventure moved too quickly. I needed time to think and work. One weekend I asked to write undistracted in my apartment, and Jerry agreed to ski in the Berkshires. The next afternoon he phoned, his voice a fading stammer. He had tumbled and broken a shoulder. With abnormal control, he drove himself to New York Hospital for an X-ray. Then, staggering up the six flights to his apartment, he felt his cheeks burn with a high fever. He'd come down with Asian influenza, the prevalent strain he studied in his laboratory.

I rushed up the landings with deli soup, bottled water, and orange juice. His face was grayish, expressionless. Sitting up to drink, he wore a white sheet like a shawl, emphasizing his helpless demeanor. He drank, took his temperature frequently, and made this request: "Either marry me or else phone every hour to check for delirium." I stayed over, welcoming the chance to make up for the many times he'd tended my family, including three sick uncles, until my mother took to calling him "a great little doctor." Late the following afternoon, he announced: "Tobin Rote is playing for Detroit against Cleveland." He was well.

His illness aroused a conflict. Would I be tending this man forever, at the expense of my freedom? Thinking that way, I left and fled down the six flights without looking back. On the bus home, I faltered. I loved him. Helping him get well came with a rush of gratification. Out the window, I saw snow starting to come down, and hail tipped with light.

One month after we met, Jerry's parents visited "his girl" in her one-room studio apartment. In the last hours of a heavy snowstorm, they drove from Brooklyn, parked blocks away, and trudged in slush. Jerry slung their wet coats over the bathroom shower rod and gave them time to settle in. His mother,

Shirley, a robust woman who shone in old family photos, handed me an immense box.

"Latkes. I made them this morning. Jerry said you'd like the way I made them."

"Oh, lovely. They will go well with the lunch I prepared." Actually, they didn't, and Jerry had readied the kosher meal, but I thought the lies might boost her confidence in me.

"Jerry passed his State Boards," I said, searching for conversation. "That means he's a board-certified internist."

"Yes, but you should meet my older son. Edward. He passed his Boards right away. They tell me they've gotten easier."

Jerry shrank in his seat. He, too, adored Edward, his mother's first and favorite doctor.

"Edward. He's handsome, like Tyrone Power. Here's his picture."

Jerry quickly asked about the drive. His father said, "Fine. I've got snow shoes," referring to tires. Car talk, a welcome relief.

"Edward's a real doctor, with patients," Shirley insisted.

The silence sat heavily. She peered around the room and cast a kind but critical gaze on the homemade bed and table. "So you don't live at home either." She stopped, meeting Jerry's frown and noticing his arm on my shoulder. "I mean this is pretty. But now Jerry, he has a nicer home with us than where he goes uptown."

Jerry's father's eyes twinkled as he supported her. "You know what Bernard said—you know, Bernard: 'It's a shame that youth is wasted on children.'"

"Meyer!" Shirley rejoined.

Jerry and I exchanged desperate glances. Shirley gestured for a hand to rescue her from the sling chair, and Jerry hoisted her up. She crossed the room to read the dozen Christmas cards I had tucked into the slats of a wood blind. In the hasty preparations for their visit, we had forgotten them. Miraculously, she turned up a card that read, "Happy Chanukah, Grandma." She turned to me with a loving smile and exclaimed, "Oh, you have a grandma!" Yes, I thought, inwardly thanking my grandma for her ethnicity. Jerry and I breathed freely. He played Brahms on the turntable. Shirley walked over and kissed me. She placed her hand on my head, as in a blessing. Then she took my hand and danced with me. We laughed. Soon after that our parents would meet and charm each other while undoubtedly expressing their common wonder as to why, given suitable homes, each of us preferred to live in close quarters.

They left. While Jerry finished the wash-up, I trekked outside to take in the cold air. The snow had tapered off, but some fluff still clung to the sleeves of coats. I studied a scraggly new pin oak in its fenced-off square of earth on University Place. Despite its enclosure, it would bloom wildly in spring. The visit had pleased me, and yet I feared the snare of family life. My days were unpredictable, theirs were expected. But could I still call myself alone? My love was losing me the resolve to go my own way.

2

ORIGINS

Jerome Schulman, who was thirty to my twenty-five, was born in Brooklyn, in Manhattan Beach near Sheepshead Bay, the second of two brothers. Their house was a short walk from the ocean, where they swam mornings before breakfast. Jerry was a young achiever, winning honors in high school and college, from class valedictorian to Phi Beta Kappa. His older brother, Edward, persuaded their parents to allow Jerry to go to Brown University, which they'd initially refused because of its distance from home. Jerry's further training was as smooth as education can be: medical school at New York University, interning at Barnes Hospital in St. Louis, a residence in internal medicine at Columbia University, New York State Boards in internal medicine. A promising young physician, he treated his patients with compassion. However, he dreamed of a career in science, to the anxiety of his parents, Polish immigrants who wanted both sons to be established doctors in their new country.

Wanting to do influenza research, he was not, at first, as promising a virologist as he was a doctor. Science was harder. And yet in 1957, a few months before we met, he gave up medical practice for scientific inquiry, the road he would take for the rest of his working life. Among the reasons he gave me, the one I best understood was his ambition to save more lives than he could by treating patients who, he said, either got well or didn't. "You were lucky, but Asian influenza has killed great numbers of people, and some of them looked like us." His emphasis on the words "killed" and "save lives" bespoke the value he placed on human existence, a principle that was to govern my thoughts.

When we met he was working in laboratories at Cornell Medical College, then a part of New York Hospital, and at the Rockefeller University. He worked under Dr. Walsh McDermott, who developed antimicrobial drugs for the treatment of tuberculosis, and who, with his wife, Marian MacPhail, an editor at *Life* magazine, became supportive friends. My only qualm was that before I'd met them, Marian had invited Jerry to meet a series of single women she worked with at *Life*. One evening they dined with us in my apartment on Jerry's fine beef stroganoff, which he served on the table he'd steadied by attaching stout wooden legs. I'd borrowed folding chairs for the occasion. They had me play the guitar, and I did, fumbling with the strings. After that dinner, Marian no longer invited Jerry without me.

Jerry's work with Drs. McDermott and René Dubos bolstered his dedication to science. From 1968 to 2006 Jerry maintained an active laboratory at Mount Sinai School of Medicine, where he conducted pioneering studies in influenza research.

One of them resulted in his discovery of the uniqueness of the Hong Kong influenza virus, which he had succeeded in differentiating from the previously prevalent Asian viruses. Hong Kong strains alone had killed an estimated one million people worldwide.

Like Jerry, I was born in Brooklyn. My parents lived uneasily with my mother's family in what I'd one day call the old house until my father's career got its start. My maternal grandfather was David Freiberger, a lawyer who founded a poetry reading series for poets from Israel, then called Palestine, at his local yeshiva. He'd arranged the passage of writers like Nathan Alterman, who camped at the Freiberger's home while in the United States. Years later, I was to think of his series as premonitory when I organized readings at the 92nd Street Y.

When David was a child, his family came to America from Hungary penniless, in search of free schools. One of twelve brothers and sisters, he attended classes in Manhattan. To save money, he walked a mile and back each day from their Lower East Side tenement to N.Y.U.'s School of Law. He married Florence, who came from a Jewish family that had resided in New York for several generations, and yet still they tried to make their old world new. They collected antiques—a silver mug, wineglasses, a Sheraton cabinet—which were held dear because they'd been owned by other Americans. In that respect, they shared affinities with the seventeenth-century Dutch burghers who commissioned Terborch portraits of their families sitting before precious objects: a spinning wheel, a crystal ewer. Florence's dreams of handing down her acquisitions through the ages stopped with me. I was not one for owning things. While I scanned museum cases for the look of rare cerulean plates, I served meals on unbreakables.

Sadly, the education of women was not among David's urgencies. From her early years his daughter, Marcella, who would become my mother, wrote poems in notebooks. Her only encouragement was the leather-bound volumes on her parents' shelves, notably Oliver Goldsmith's verses and the King James Bible. Her wish for formal learning met with light-hearted dismissal. Florence, who was inclined to move whenever her living quarters required repainting, found houses near schools for boys, rather than for girls, requiring Marcella to walk far, alone, to classes. When David moved wife and daughter to the Azores in his post as a legal consultant for a Portuguese pineapple factory, his two sons remained in college at home. Marcella, my despairing mother, was taken out of high school to join her parents abroad. Much later she continued her education at Columbia University's School of General Studies. However, to her lasting regret, she never matriculated for a degree. And only when it was time to fill out my own college applications did she shamefully confess that she was never allowed to finish high school.

David's sympathies were ample. As a lawyer, he visited convicts he did not know in Sing Sing prison, bringing gifts and offering to contact their relatives. In Portugal, he befriended the factory owner's son, and brought him to live with the family in America. So, too, he indulged his sons. But Marcella strained under his harness.

When David and Florence returned to Brooklyn, they were not prepared for Marcella's errant new love, and less so for her declaration to wed. My parents met at a party, which was acceptable, though her choice was not. My father, Bernard Waldman, a Polish Jew, was cultivated by stays in Germany and in England. In Berlin he trained as an actor at the Reichersche Hochschule für Dramatische Kunst, performing odd jobs for tuition, and received a graduation certificate signed by the conservatory's director, Friedrich Moest. In England in 1919, he found occasional work as an actor while waiting for a ship to take him to America. He boarded the R.M.S. *Berengaria* second class, on December 29, 1922, and did recitations from Ibsen to subsidize his passage. In New York, he gathered a little group of actors called the Gotham Players, in a studio at 51 West Twelfth Street, and produced plays by Ibsen, Strindberg, and a newcomer, Alice E. Ives.

He was an actor out of work when he met my mother. He studied law at City College, was graduated, and passed the bar exam, but gave that up soon after. "I'd imagined pleading before the bar, and it wasn't like that. It was about settling out of court." When my parents eloped, in 1928, he started an advertising agency at David's urging. "If you marry that actor, you'll live in terrible need," my grandfather reportedly had said. At his agency my father took to graphics, and to designing posters like those he had seen in the London Underground. His love for the theater remained undiminished: he and my mother took me, from age seven, to see plays with actors such as puckish John Garfield as Peer Gynt and vivacious Helen Hayes as Queen Victoria. My earliest theater memory is of an actor ranting as King Lear. I was drawn to the mistreated king when, in the storm scene, he touched his head for a crown no longer there. Then, seeing the swords clashing for his throne, I suddenly thought they were real. I cried softly for Lear, and

my father passed me his handkerchief. His smile told me that
he was not concerned but amused. I'd been transported.

My mother worked for his agency, writing fashion copy
for magazine advertisements. She complained of her anonymity
as she sat typing phrases in the back room. The job was never
to nourish her gift for writing poetry, but it consumed her,
using her wordsmithing skill. And in her surroundings, it was
common for married women to adapt, like her crony Harriet
Trilling, sister of Lionel, the critic and novelist. Harriet was a
trained soprano who gave up her career to assist her husband,
Roland Schwartz, a dentist with an office in our building.
When she spoke I heard anger in her gentle tones.

My mother's diversion was wordplay. She would teach
me "lion" from "dandelion" and read from Shakespeare while
reminding me that I was born on his birthday. On her manual
typewriter, she showed me how to type my earliest poems
and kept them in her own three-ring notebook. One Saturday
I memorized a Hopi rain prayer I'd read in one of her books,
and chanted it so that we could stay at home and play words.
In serious moments, she taught me to cherish independence,
a woman's best hope of survival. "You can do whatever you
want—if you don't give in to someone's view of who you are."
She was to repeat it, changing the wording, but with the same
emphasis.

When I was two months old, my parents moved to
Manhattan, where I grew up at 20 West Eighty-Sixth Street, on
a block that has not changed much in half a century. Revisiting
now, I see only a few alterations: a bank; a Gap where our
soda-fountain drugstore had been; and a copy center in place
of the old florist. Otherwise, there are the same tall apartment

buildings with doormen, one of them home, and the same white sandstone houses we erroneously called "brownstones." On the side streets were truly brown buildings, private houses divided into apartments. In one of the white houses on our block was my "progressive" private high school, Bentley, now gone to a condominium.

Nature was Central Park, half a block away from our house. Before high school, I was allowed to go there only with an elder. I was an only child, used to being solitary, but when taken to the park I bounded for the crowded swings in the "little-children's playground," and later, for the roller-skating rink. I climbed what I fantasized were mountains set with diamonds, actually small rocks inlaid with mica. My grandfather, who had slighted my mother as a child, doted on me. He took me to the park, to the zoo, and to see Laurel and Hardy movies on Forty-Second Street. I lived for his visits, usually on Saturdays. "Don't send her to school, I'll teach her myself" was a plea my mother ignored, a tune she'd heard before.

At five years old, I came down with an infection of the eyelids that left me unable to see. There being no effective treatment in those pre-antibiotic days, the blindness dragged on into summer, fall, and winter. After trying useless remedies, my family resorted to warm-water soaks, which sometimes revealed daylight. Unfortunately, my parents were away: my father went to Hollywood periodically for a project he'd invented called Cinema Fashions, which would bring copies of dresses worn in movies to retail stores. My mother, whether bending to his wishes or fearing to shake her marriage, joined him. She was to write a story about a woman who watched her husband kissing a starlet. When I read it as an adult,

I understood her early anxiety.

I was cared for lavishly at my grandparents' in Brooklyn.

Two uncles taught me to "see" by feeling the textures
of toys. I couldn't get enough of my uncle Josh, who played
Portuguese fados on the mandolin. My grandmother coaxed
my appetite for meals, and brought me a chocolate-and-vanilla
Dixie cup whenever we heard the ice-cream wagon's bell-like
tunes on the street. My grandfather read to me from *The Folk
Tales of All Nations*, a book he inscribed to me in an arresting
Gothic script, "To Grace Waldman from her grandfather,
David Freiberger," even though he knew I couldn't read it.
"Now comes the story," he would read, and no one else could
say it as he did. Edward Lear's "The Owl and the Pussycat"
was a favorite of mine, and he read it repeatedly in a wide
range of tones. I remember those months as a seesaw of joy
and sorrow, up for the attention I got, down for the parents I
missed. Up for the relatives constantly at my side, down for the
frustration of not reading for myself. Down with a bump for
the passing of time. I could not tell the hours.

After nine months, I recovered. I woke one morning and
cried aloud when I saw light come through the windows, saw
the windows, saw my grandfather, saw the books he read from.
I went to a public school in Manhattan, the first grade taught
by Miss McGee. I did well, equipped with the words and numbers I'd been taught. But after being confined and attended
by grownups, I was restless in the company of other children. "Works and Plays Well with Others" got me low marks.
Thereafter, I acted the role. I found a friend, and we even
skipped rope at recess, but the wish for solitude stayed on.

My grandfather died of a stroke when I turned fourteen.

I was in Nags Head, North Carolina, on vacation from school with my uncle Josh's then-current fiancée, Pepi. I'd talked her into it, secretly wanting to go there because I was taken with the drawl of a boy from the South. We had come from a swim when my father phoned and said, "Sweetheart, Pop died." I reeled in disbelief—how could he die?—and we rode home on the train. My mother was hosting her aunts who burst into sobs at the sight of me walking in the door. My uncle Milton, who'd had a severe mental breakdown, wailed. The family went into such turmoil over the settling of my grandfather's estate that Pepi, my Uncle Josh's love, said she couldn't tolerate the mess and disappeared.

In my high-school years at Bentley, I'd wander, usually alone, inside the Hayden Planetarium and the Museum of Natural History, both majestic structures near my home. In walking distance was the Ethical Culture Society, an angular, solemn-looking building where, on Sundays, I woke to the "faith without creeds" sermons of Algernon Black, the Society's leader and a founder of the Experiment in International Living, a group for working abroad. In his sermons he asserted that you could do religious acts without going to a house of worship, a belief that still lingers in me.

At the Society I square-danced with a classmate, Alex Alland. One day he walked the mile home with me to Eighty-Sixth Street singing folk songs of Burl Ives, such as "Wayfaring Stranger" and "Black Is the Color." Our class sang them on our field trip to rural Maryland, where we biked to 4-H youth clubs and met teenagers whose farm ways were very different from our city habits. To bridge the gaps, we sang Appalachian ballads. We all knew them.

I was not a diligent student at Bentley. My distraction was an older man. It began with a need for assurance. I'd been distressed by my size, thin as a blade and uncommonly tall. Even my exact measurement had the awkward sound of "five feet eleven and three-quarters inches." I had to recite it often, because classmates asked my height even before they knew my name. My mother was concerned and let me know it. Teachers identified me as "that tall girl." Feeling that way, I suffered when I saw Tenniel's illustration of Alice in Wonderland, fallen down the rabbit hole and stretched out tall as a giant.

Once, at a school dance where girls wore satin dresses with suede pumps, I strapped on sandals with flat heels I'd pried off to be even flatter, the nails clawing through. I paled when the teacher thought up a game: girls would pile shoes in the center of a ring, and each boy would pick a shoe and dance with its owner. Stealthily I tucked mine under the heap of suede or patent-leather shells with curvy insteps, hoping that some prospective suitor might see through it to the me myself. But no, my ragged heelless sandal remained unclaimed. I was a poor version of Cinderella, with no prince in sight. And then I was done for: the teacher hoisted my elongated shoe above her head as though it were a dead centipede, demanding, "Whose is this?" No need to ask again. I ran home barefoot in the rain, skidding on wet pavement.

Everything changed at sixteen, when I met Robert, who was my senior by nine years and at least as tall, at my grandfather's funeral. His straight, tan hair fell forward when he spoke, and he swept it back in the manner of Farley Granger, a movie star I'd seen in *Strangers on a Train*. He had just finished his medical internship, and I was charmed to learn that he was the son of the doctor who delivered me. Better still, I could meet him after school and brush past the girls who disparaged my height. Best of all, he'd read Lord Byron's poems at Harvard, and could quote the whole first stanza of "She Walks in Beauty." He took me to the movies and, once, to a play, Rostand's *Cyrano de Bergerac*, with José Ferrer. He called me his long-legged girl. And although it would take me years to have good sex, this was a caring introduction to it.

The little romance didn't last long, but in the heat of it I found in the school library a book covered in worn gray cloth, an anthology of sonnets from Wyatt through Thomas Hardy. "I am a little world, made cunningly / of Elements" were lines that flamed and roared. While I wasn't sure of their meaning, the sounds of the words, and their urgency, had me enthralled. It was snowing outside, the streets white, the people vanishing before ghostlike buildings, and what I held in my hands was feeling and thought clearly defined in black print. John Donne was a name I said over and over, as though wanting to talk with him. I showed the poem to a teacher who read it aloud to me. Next day she showed me how to construct a sonnet, and I wrote one a day for at least a year. As a senior, I sent the whole sheaf along with my application to Bard College, and was accepted despite my indifferent grades.

Those years were not unhappy, but restricting. There were tight rules for dress and social behavior, laid out as evenly as the geometric blocks. When I grew old enough to take the subway alone, I rode downtown to Greenwich Village. I walked on streets that curved and deviated and crossed themselves, West Fourth meeting West Fourth. I went to a café called the Figaro and sat at a table with an open chessboard waiting for players.

I stared at the game my mother had taught me. A woman sat at my table, across from me. I wondered what to say to her. No need. Without a word, she held out a hand offering me black or white. I chose, and we began our moves. I was free.

3

TWISTED BRANCHES

Marriage was not my only conflict in 1957. I was torn between my passion for poetry and the wish to report news. Earlier, the course had seemed predictable: school, college, work. Marriage could wait, perhaps forever.

As long as I can remember, I was fascinated and overwhelmed by elders. While my mother urged me to seek others my age, the Bentley schoolgirls talked mostly of eyelash makeup and (yes, really) new fur coats. Grown into adolescence, I preferred to relax and listen to the witty conversations of my parents' friends, whether or not I could understand them.

Monroe Wheeler was among them. At the time he served as director of exhibitions for the Museum of Modern Art. He amused me with tales of seeking art in France, and I pictured him among artists and patrons laughing in a field of yellow flowers like the one in a Matisse canvas. His sophisticated anecdotes went beyond me, but he didn't condescend: once, responding to my interest in modern art, he invited me to his office. I was elated. When I left, he had the elevator stop at floor two for my free visit to the Picassos.

His longtime partner, Glenway Wescott, was a writer I knew I could not dare to emulate. I found his novel *The Pilgrim Hawk* on my parents' shelves, took down the book with its worn red cover, and tried to picture his characters in a great French house far away. Once, in a restaurant, Glenway turned to me and said, in no context whatever, "Monroe and I have not had sex since 1929." I was startled, still a child, and before coming out was routine. My father looked quizzical, and I didn't know whether it was in response to the subject or to the length of abstinence.

Through Wheeler, we met E. McKnight (Ted) Kauffer, a painter who worked with my father designing posters for American Airlines. Kauffer, who was born in Montana, had lived in London, where he illustrated T. S. Eliot's *Ariel* editions, a series that included "Marina" and "Journey of the Magi." He had come back to his native country in 1940, after the outbreak of World War II. As a family friend, he gave me books he'd illustrated, boxed sets of *Green Mansions* and *The Anatomy of Melancholy*. When I asked him for a book that would help me be a writer, he gave me *Webster's Dictionary*, desk edition. As with Wheeler's stories, at fourteen I was intrigued but abashed at my meager understanding of the words in those fine editions.

Kauffer and my father believed in making no distinction between fine art and applied art, and the painter happily illustrated a promotional pamphlet on fashion called "Paris" for Brighton Mills, a fabrics manufacturer. It was my mother's discomfort that troubled me. When I grew old enough to judge her writing, she showed me a passage in her little book, some-

thing about a redingote—long, double-breasted, full—worn by
a model at the Louvre.

"Do you like it?" she asked, searching for approval, aware
that her fashion copy fell below her aesthetic reach. "What
about the language? Is it written well?" Of course I praised
it, but silently obeyed, even at sixteen, the sharp distinction
between service to commerce and service to a higher power.
The coat she adorned with hard-won phrases would give way
to a shorter one the following season.

My mother knew it. All the while she wrote uncredited, she
wanted to sign her work and address a more permanent audience. I felt it was her marriage that kept her from it, although
she wouldn't have put it that way. In my view she wore a
mask, and her face shone through occasionally, with regret
that she had sacrificed her talent for a man's career, her ambition shunted into serviceable forms. As early as 1953, before
the feminist protests, she nailed to the kitchen wall, partly
hidden from sight, a framed cover of Ashley Montagu's book
The Natural Superiority of Women. Ashley had given it to her,
unframed. He, too, was a frequent visitor. My father met him
while taking classes at the University of London. Paradoxically,
she'd half concealed his title with a houseplant. She was not
accorded that superiority.

Although my father held the advertising agency until
he died in 1980, he was constantly torn between principle
and submission to clients. Once he visited a factory owner in
Georgia, heard racial disparagements of carders and weavers,
and slurs against a Jewish partner. At dinner, he was invited
to say grace, a custom his host extended to guests. After a long
pause, he pulled a white handkerchief out of his pocket, knot-

ted the corners, clapped it on his head, and uttered:

Baruch atah Adonai eloheinu melech ha olam . . .

He looked up at an amused but startled company, and finished the prayer.

For him it was not always that simple. For me his was a directive to hold fast, which has served me as a poet in a sometimes dismissive world.

An irresistible attraction was Frances Steloff, founder of the Gotham Book Mart in the Diamond District of Manhattan. Frances had started it in 1920 as a literary haven, selling copies of D. H. Lawrence's banned *Lady Chatterley's Lover*. My father took me there for meetings of the James Joyce Society, where we heard talks by the Irish writer Padraic Colum and, once, scenes from *Finnegan's Wake* read by the actor Siobhán McKenna. My father gave a talk on Leopold Bloom of *Ulysses,* referring to the history of Jews in Ireland.

A smiling woman with a cloud of white hair, Frances sat on a child-size wooden rocker in a small alcove, and greeted my father by kissing him on the mouth. "If I had a father like yours, I'd be floating," she declared. I wasn't sure what she meant, but liked it, nonetheless. After Andreas Brown bought the store in 1967, she remained as a consultant. In my teens I'd thrill to my father's purchases of her selections for me.

Once Frances took me to a lecture by Joseph Campbell on myth and human experience. Afterwards I wanted to thank him. "How long did it take you to write that?" was all I could blurt out. "One day," he replied kindly. Seeing my surprise, he added: "But—I did nothing else." One of her visitors from abroad was Yukio Mishima, the Japanese author of *Five Modern*

Noh Plays, as the first edition was called. At his book-signing in 1957, he inscribed one to me in Japanese ideograms. His language, translated by Donald Keene, swept me into a world of ordinary characters, a cop, a dancer, a salesclerk; and images such as a damask drum that made no sound. Joking in a fluent, fast-wforward English, a mixture of high diction and slang, Mishima was a princely man, conservatively dressed in jacket-and-tie. He was to shock the world in 1970 by committing hara-kiri publicly, in protest against a new Japanese constitution forbidding war. I would not have guessed from his cordiality, and his fine, earthy plays, that he was a martyr to the "samurai way."

Among these elders, the only visitor who did not intimidate me was Marianne Moore, whom my parents met through Ted Kauffer, the designer of one of her books. When I was fourteen, Ted Kauffer and his wife, Marion Dorn, invited me to lunch with her in their apartment at 40 Central Park South. They said she was a great poet. I was struck by the combination of her humility and gorgeous vocabulary. I liked her humor, ranging from deadpan to high comedy. She told of swallowing a capsule whose red dye stained her blouse. Writing a complaint to the pharmaceutical company, she asked "If the dye has medicinal value, why not put it *inside* the capsule?" Inspired by her and by Glenway Wescott, I wrote my first poems and sent them to her. She wrote back, "The flawless typing shows the work to its very best advantage and is in itself a great pleasure." It was my introduction to her way of dodging a negative response. She spoke truth tactfully, and with a positive spin.

Even before we became friends, I'd delighted in hearing about how she'd joined my parents at their favorite restaurant, La Caravelle, on West Fifty-Fifth Street. She wore a new red suit, and beamed when they noticed it. Once, my father took her to Moskowitz and Lupowitz, now vanished, an elegant Romanian restaurant on Second Avenue and Second Street. Guided by my father, Miss Moore enjoyed chopped liver, stuffed derma, and fricassee. Introduced to the headwaiter, she said, "Please give my compliments to Mrs. Moskowitz."

With some others, I felt an outsider. Flying above my head were pointed words, some in bold type, for emphasis. They evoked laughter, relaying judgments about books, theater, and people. Not so with Marianne Moore. She spoke slowly, and her observations were meaningful. I listened intently as she said, "I walked through masses of bloom today in the park, white and pink cherry blossoms." I woke to her verbs, as when she declared, of Anne Novak, my father's longtime assistant, "I *venerate* that girl." And to her metaphors, as in, "I've been beaten down this week. My nerves are in an eggbeater." For my parents, she became a friend; for me, she was a steady light.

I visited Miss Moore often, on Cumberland Street in Brooklyn and then on Ninth Street in Manhattan. I wore my longest skirts because initially, when raised hemlines were in, she had said, eyeing my bare knees, "Grace, you are so *fashionable*." I knew from her intonation how she felt about above-the-knee skirts, and made changes in my wardrobe. On one of the visits, speaking of her poems, she said, "I write in response to adverse ideas." I read many of her poems with that in mind, noting that they begin with a response to an idea she debates: a quotation from a newspaper article, a poem, a friend. The tone of argument intrigued me, drew me into the poem. Eventually the idea developed into a book I wrote about her poetry of argument, *Marianne Moore: The Poetry of Engagement*.

I continued to write poetry despite the fear of disappointing my seniors. At Bard College, I felt a failure when my poems were judged not good enough for Harvey Shapiro's workshop. "Schoolgirl poems," he said, placing his coffee mug on the sheaf I'd given him. Annoyed by the brown stains, I went to the college library, open round the clock with plush armchairs, and worked through the night to write for Harvey. After I slipped them in his mailbox, he waved at me on campus and said, "I liked your poems."

But it was too late. I resolved to move on. Since starting Bard I'd hidden my longing for news writing. Secretly, I was drawn to journalism because it was outside my family's ken, and therefore immune to their advice and help. Also, I was drawn to events that needed reporting. The first was my encounter with the brave general Humberto Delgado. He came to my family from José Bensaude, the Portuguese factory-owner's son who had lived with my grandparents.

Delgado opposed the fascist government of Prime Minister António de Oliveira Salazar, whose regime violated liberties from free speech to minimal attire, even on beaches. In protest, furious at the "proper clothing" rules, Delgado ran into the sea wearing a top hat, white tie, and tails. When he proposed an opposition candidate, Henrique Galvão, Delgado was exiled and Galvão imprisoned. Some years later, the general returned to Portugal and was shot.

He moved me, this man with slick black hair, coal eyes,

and, despite bleakness, humor. I tried repeatedly to write a poem about his plight, and realized that only journalism could convey his suffering. I was determined to train as a reporter.

It was a trip to Israel, though, that turned the key. At nineteen, while still at Bard, I visited my father's parents, who had escaped from Poland before Hitler's rise to power. In Ramat Gan I met my grandmother, seemingly frail, who could handle a rifle and who fed chickens on her farm, talking to them in Hebrew and French. My *sabta*, as I learned to call her, wore high-topped lace-up boots in the style of Al Capp's Mammy Yokum, mother of *Li'l Abner*.

I traveled with a student group lodged at Beit Berl College in Kfar Saba. The Arab village of Qalkilya was within shouting—and shooting—distance. The border, which I could see, was a scene of bloodshed in a constant war. I had to go there.

Borders summoned me. As a child, visiting my mother's parents in Brooklyn, I had a playmate with bright yellow hair that I liked better than my own brown curls. She lived across the street, beyond a white road divider. One day her mother called us in from play, washed our faces, and had me tell my grandmother that she was taking us to church to see the bride. "No, and stay on your side," I was told. That white road divider burned in me like a scar.

Stay on your side or be shot. I could not obey. While others had lunch in Kfar Saba, I set out for the border. It was irresistible. As I came near, three Arabs in keffiyeh headdress waved at me to cross. They cast sidelong glances at my bare legs in shorts and my loose windblown hair. One of them offered me a cigar, an English brand. We spoke in French. I remembered the Israelis' warnings—*Don't walk that path. They shoot you*—but ventured farther. On my side of the border were date palms, on theirs, white sand. *There's rifle-fire at night.* We chatted until I realized I had crossed the forbidden border. *La frontière.* I turned to leave. He extended a hand.

"Stay a while longer."

"They told me there's been fighting here," I ventured nervously.

My new friend smiled and said, "Yes, but you see, we don't become enemies until six o'clock at night." He changed it, glancing discreetly at my wristwatch: "Well, maybe six-thirty."

Callow I was, but the experience remained in my adult life as a comment on the nonsense of war, the tissue-thin covering of hostility over the human instinct for cordiality. That day I got back safely, but was reproachfully told that three soldiers had been killed on the same path.

One evening in Kfar Saba a handsome sabra came to visit the school—slim green shorts, strong thighs, intense blue eyes—and we talked until sunset. In time, we walked through the village and hitchhiked through Israel, a common mode of transportation. We stopped overnight at a kibbutz in Caesarea, where archaeologists were excavating a temple. We visited my grandparents in Ramat Gan, where, oddly, my grandmother prepared one big bed for us to sleep in, just as they had done in the kibbutz.

Sharing a bed was a custom based on the housing shortage.

It was not an invitation to have sex, nor did we take it as one. We were too amazed—to see the kibbutz farmers at work, to see the country whizzing by from the backs of hay wagons. I was no stranger to sex, having been initiated by the older

doctor I'd met when in high school. But this chaste affair was
a different matter. Every day Rafi picked a flower for me from
a roadside shrub. He was courtly, affectionate, and undemanding. After I left Israel, I never saw Rafi again, but we corre-
sponded. With his permission I used his picture in an article I
wrote, and my father sent to his friend at the *Berkeley Carteret*,
then a New Jersey newspaper. It was my first publication.

After Delgado, after Israel, I wanted to experience the
world's dangers and come through them whole. I left Bard to
finish college in Washington, D.C., and, because of my article,
was hired as an intern at the Jewish Telegraphic Agency. After
college, I worked on an afternoon daily newspaper, covering
the police, the federal court, schools, and the sanitation authority. The *Alexandria Gazette* was located in a rickety wooden
building in its Virginia city. Reporters stood on line to use the
few standard typewriters with faded ribbons. The day's stories
were written against the din of the in-house Linotype machines
and the city editor's shouts for prompt copy. Sometimes he
grabbed the page I worked on and tugged it out of my typewriter. I kept longer hours for less pay than the men on the
staff, struggling to justify my gender in a newsroom, and was
often asked to fetch coffee for them.

Even so, my assignments were absorbing. At federal court
I covered the trial of a man accused of espionage; and at civil
court I scribbled notes about a woman convicted of murdering
her small children. In 1954, when the Supreme Court decision *Brown v. Board of Education* came on the tickers, I pulled
out tapes from the Associated Press: segregation of schools—
beaches—restaurants—theaters—libraries—with "all deliber-
ate speed." The news meant school integration in Alexandria.

My best breaks were storms. Things happened in the hospital, on the streets. Once when my mother, in New York, read that a hurricane raged through Northern Virginia, she phoned the *Gazette* to find out if I was safe. "She's safely out covering the hurricane," the city editor told her.

When I returned to New York, I found that women were seldom hired on newspapers. "Can I put a pretty girl like you on a night desk?" a managing editor asked even after he'd seen, on my résumé, that I'd worked on one for a year. After many tries, I gave up covering news for a job writing about books and records for *Glamour* magazine. Located in the Graybar Building, on Forty-Second Street, the office was hospitable to the woman beginning a career. Jill Krementz, a research assistant, showed me a camera she had received as a gift, and said she'd experiment with it after work. Elsewhere in the Graybar, Joan Didion sat typing her articles for *Vogue*. More numerous were the fashion editors, who wore stiletto heels, cursed in French, and spoke in italics to stress chosen words.

Something was missing. Before long, I was writing poems again. I knew I had to decide between alternatives, to live in one place or another, to stay on one side of the dangerous border or to venture off. In that restless period, my life resembled an oak in Central Park whose branches splayed out in many directions, south, north, east, west. At times I sat under the oak and stared upward through a tangled mass of leaves to blue sky. Now I stood puzzled before crooked branches.

As to wedlock, I heard the stress on "lock." I could not consider a settled existence, certainly not in the staid 1950s with its fixed gender roles. Nor could I let go of a life-changing love, the tree trunk from which all branches grew.

4

HIGH NOON

When it came to marriage, I could delay Jerry no longer than two years. "Look, we are married in every way. Why not make it official? We'll work, strum, walk, fight. Same difference," he declared one day. I loved him but still feared the confines of wedded life. Freedom, my mother had taught, was the highest choice, never to be endangered. Jerry had a direction in his work, while I was still seeking one.

I needed to think. In a cold February, in 1959, I packed a small bag, put on a winter coat, and left for Barcelona with thirty dollars in my wallet, enough to cover a five-night stay in a rooming house just a short walk from Antoni Gaudí's Sagrada Familia church. Without unpacking, I went to a park nearby and sat on a bench alone. Musicians were playing wooden flutes. Soon a crowd gathered and formed a circle. Hands were everywhere, and feet stepped to the sardana, a local folk dance. I joined the dance, amiable people inviting me into their ring. With each turn I felt free—but with each counter-turn

I wished that Jerry were dancing there with me. I came home resolved never to leave him. And finally, when I returned home he convinced me that by marriage he meant not a protective shelter—not a house, not even a tent, but a common path through dense trees.

I would change my name to his, Grace Waldman to Grace Schulman. The loss was chilling: would I lose my self just as I was seeking it? But I knew it would have confused employers, registrars, and professors in an age unused to wives with maiden names. The only time I tried being a wife named Grace Waldman, I was met with a baffled stare: "Do you mean you married a Waldman?"

We were wed at the Plaza Hotel on September 6, 1959. I was twenty-seven to his thirty-two. His parents, Conservative Jews, had to adjust to our Reform wedding, with no canopy and no bridal veil. His mother had assumed that the groom would ritually step on a glass, but our Rabbi Bamberger discouraged it: "We don't know the exact reason for it, and the breakage could be dangerous." His parents did, however, compliment the rabbi on his address, which emphasized the separateness inherent in a good marriage. Jerry's brother, Edward, flew in from Boston to be best man. With him was his wife, Beatrice, large with her second child. My mother helped me pick out a silky beige dress. She herself wore an outsize blue one, my father fearing she would look too sexy if she wore her true size. I was marrying the man I loved, and Jerry was beaming. In other words, a perfect day.

Why then did I pace the dressing room and down four cups of strong black coffee?

I'm stricken with terror. And what am I doing now? What

if I lose my freedom? What if it doesn't work? What would that do to my grandmother? Surely a divorce would give her cause for vast concern. Step back, now: what if he is summoned to a lab in Texas? What would I do there? My father smiles reassuringly as he walks me down the aisle, but my hands are shaking. The bridesmaid, my cousin Katie, is shooting me a doubtful glance. The makeshift altar is raised too high on too steep a platform. I can't see the rabbi, let alone climb up to where he stands. My white rose bouquet has wilted. The rabbi speaks mostly in English, but his few Hebrew words seem an admonition for me to be as loyal as Ruth to my mother-in-law. The pianist is playing funereal music. The tradition calls forth high moral standards, the prayers assuming spotless behavior, and I think we might not come up to the mark.

Responding to my voice, which quivered as we exchanged vows, Jerry felt that what we needed was freedom. After the reception, we sank into the Austin-Healey and drove far into upstate New York. We had no itinerary, no reservations. We'd forgotten it was Labor Day, and hotel vacancies were scarce. Around midnight we found a room, though we had to sleep in separate beds. No matter. Whatever the inconvenience, we were glad to have done it off the cuff.

Encouraged by that impromptu procedure, we left the following week for Turkey, Greece, France, and Spain, with no agenda, and we breathed free. Jerry and I would continue to travel impulsively and without reservations throughout our marriage. And, though I didn't know it, my wedding panic would prove groundless. We were to stay married forever.

After the plane ride, our only fixed plan was Jerry's virology convention in Istanbul, and even there we had no booking. Rooms were scarce, but when Jerry revealed our nuptials to a clerk, we were given a suite with a view of the Bosporus and Dardanelles straits. We had arranged a two-week break from our jobs, but extended our stay toward the end. When an Air France desk clerk shouted at our attempt to change the unchangeable tickets, Jerry quieted his tirade by studying his nervous behavior, saying, "I suspect a hyperthyroidism that you might want to check out." As usual, his calm, logical manner cleared the air.

In Turkey we saw light pouring through the windowed dome of Hagia Sophia and looked up at it. "It's called Holy Wisdom for the way it changes its mind," Jerry said, referring to how the structure had gone from a Greek Orthodox basilica to Catholic cathedral to mosque to the museum we lingered in. I applauded his whimsy. None of my traveling before—alone, or with the spy, or with Rafi—had been half so compelling.

In Greece we walked from central Athens to the suburb of Dafni for a wine festival, and joined a line of dancers, following their steps. Always we were alike in obeying impulses, valuing the same places, and wanting to walk everywhere we could for contact with foreign earth. When we climbed Delphi, regretting that we hadn't time for the islands, we ran unexpectedly into a neighbor, who suggested Hydra, for its nearness to Athens. So we set off on the ferry, carrying only one small valise and a larger tape recorder, a reel-to-reel, that my father had given us as a wedding present. We used it to record folk songs of other nations, which we had been collecting since that day in the Square.

A stalwart man in a white suit helped us haul the tape

recorder onto the ferry, then sat facing us. When told the
recorder's purpose, he sang a chorus of "Meidani," a song he
knew from childhood about a shepherdess, and said the words
slowly, spelling them out for me to write them down. Very
soon he, Ianos, confided that he was running from a love affair.
He amused us with assertions such as "Love is like democracy.
To each his own conception." I felt for his aloneness, glad that
I had my love and that Jerry and I had mutual "conceptions."
Ianos was booked for a long trip. We left him to disembark at
our dock, happy to have won a new friendship, however brief,
so soon after our marriage.

Hydra was exhilarating. Jerry and I dived from high rocks
into the Aegean, then climbed 210 steps (I counted them) up
a mountain stair to our hotel, a bare, white, high-ceilinged
structure that cast sharp, black shadows on the rock in bright
sunlight. There we dried off under the open arches that served
for windows. Evenings we descended to the harbor and chose
a café for our dinners of souvlaki and ouzo, then up again to
the whitewashed house, gazing at stars as large as baseballs in
the night sky. Inside, alone together, the only guests in that
house, we drank Metaxa, a smooth amber brandy, and sang a
song called "Papalambrena." Hearing a musician play it on a
six-stringed bouzouki in an Athens nightclub, we'd learned
the words we didn't understand and went over the melody
until we could sing it at will.

Our only uneasy moment came when we found no soap in
the shower stall, the hotelier gone, and no neighbors in sight.
Because of the scarcity of spoken English, we valued communication all the more for the work it required. We began to
cherish the words we'd taken for granted. Next day, in the only

harbor store, Jerry gestured for soap in a shower pantomime. When that didn't work, he tried possible words. "Sopa, soupa" he said. Suddenly a voice issued from the back room and a comely young woman appeared. "No," she said, her English tinged with a scholarly intonation, "*soupa* is soup. You want *sapouni*." Jerry shrugged. In later years, much as we lauded Hydra, we vowed never to go back when the tourists discovered it. In our time, the scant population caused us to turn inward, strangers in a strange land, and gain a deeper sense of ourselves.

In Hydra we looked death in the face. Or was it life at its highest elevation? One day, having coffee in a harbor café, we watched a gray cutter pull into the harbor, the vessel towering above the fishing boats. We learned it was transporting a fisherman who died in Athens to burial at home. A priest carrying a wooden cross led a procession to the pier. A crowd gathered, the women wearing long black garments and pacing the ground like crows. When the ship docked, swimmers and fishermen in the harbor stood solemnly, a silent chorus, as the mourners followed the coffin up the mountain. We were hallowing an ordinary man, not a naval hero, not Odysseus, not someone we knew. Jerry's swim trunks were still wet, his tall lean figure unmoving. "We stand for his life, not for his death," Jerry said. He could have added, as we do for our lives, at high noon.

In Paris we knew we'd have to extend our wedding trip. We booked in a cheap hotel—small room, bathroom outside — on the Rue Jacob, a short distance from one of Sartre's cafés, the Flore. The single lamp was dim, and I reckoned that the writers who worked in cafés did so not only to keep warm but for the light. Over croissants at Café de Flore and Les Deux Magots, I scribbled notes while Jerry wrote equations, lines of x's, y's, and raised numerals. From there we strode down the Boulevard Saint-Germain to gape at statues of French queens in the Luxembourg Garden. In a rush of happiness, we walked down the Boulevard Saint-Michel to the Seine and crossed a bridge to hear a sublime performance of Fauré's Requiem at the Église Saint-Louis-en-l'Île. At night we hiked to the Lapin Agile in Montmartre and heard songs of the Auvergne, so many I thought the people of that region must be singing day and night. Our faces reddened in candle flame as we heard a muscular bass deliver "Old Man River." I flushed with excitement when I remembered reading that Jean-Paul Sartre sang it to win a woman. But the most endearing moment was at L'Orientais, a subterranean jazz dive, when we heard Juliette Gréco, a chanteuse with long straight hair and sparkling black eyes, sing a love song, "Je me souviens de tout."

As I write I can still hear her voice, of long, turning phrases, arabesques, and a flawless tone. Closing her set, she sang "L'Ombre" ("Shadow"), the music composed to a poem by François Mauriac that haunts me still. It was of a day when the sun was so close to the earth that trees burned, streams dried up, and only the crickets were heard. On that day, she moaned, *I searched for your heart as I searched for a shadow.*

Those words cut deep when I read the poignant story that she and Miles Davis, the great jazz trumpeter, had been in love. They sat in cafés with Sartre, and, young and carefree, ran down Saint-Germain. While Paris accepted the romance of a white French woman and a black American, New York would not. Eventually he had to leave for his country, both of them knowing they did not belong in each other's worlds.

Saddened by their fate, I wanted them to belong to the same world, and I knew now that Jerry and I did. With independent lives, we had each other. Our marriage fortified us and brightened our days just as our separateness was a new kind of freedom. More than once I told myself, "I've chosen this. My choice made me what I am, and what I will become."

5

THE CHOICE

*B*oth of us together, each apart, began a prayer in our marriage ceremony. Our rabbi had spoken it in English. After the wedding, I heard the words in my head. They reminded me of a paper I'd written on Jean-Paul Sartre, inspired by his book, *L'Être et le néant*, later translated as *Being and Nothingness*. It was for a graduate class at Johns Hopkins University, which had provided nourishing support between my work on the *Gazette* and my return to New York. I became initiated into Sartre's belief that you are alone, with complete freedom of choice, and what you choose becomes what you are. Despite its happy sound, freedom is terrible because of the entire responsibility for each choice among alternatives. The affirmative side is that consciousness is achieved in that way, since it is a realization of being "for itself." "This is true," I'd said.

His idea stayed true for us all of our married lives. Frequently, I'd hear Jerry speak of an "existential sin," referring to passivity, his own or someone else's, in making a choice. Once he went so far as to say "People think that money determines what they do. It doesn't. Nothing does, except what you choose." He, too, believed in Sartre's call for the action required to change your present state.

Marianne Moore, who had never married, was, ironically, the wedding guest in 1959 who brought me back from a state of panic. At the reception, she asked, "Are you happy?" Then, reading my silence and skeptical expression, she changed the subject to praise the language she'd heard. "The rabbi gave you both the responsibility," she said, and I thought of how close her view was to Sartre's ideology. Not God, I thought, not fate, imagining what she did not say. Moore told us that her brother, a Presbyterian minister and chaplain, would have enjoyed our wedding.

"There is no fear in love," she had said to me once. I thought of her pure belief, knowing that she had doubts but always returned to the wisdom of the Scriptures. When she quoted the Bible, I was certain the comfort she derived was in the heightened language.

My particular Jewish faith gave me more of an intellectual heritage than a religious one. I sensed that my parents wished for belief but never attained it, for they were long on Jewish identification and short on ritual. I had one of the earliest bat mitzvahs in New York, so early that people didn't understand the term. They argued that I must have meant *bar* mitzvah, and that only boys had them. Weary of explaining, I fell quiet and affirmed my gender within me. The bat mitzvah took place at the Society for the Advancement of Judaism, a Reconstructionist temple on the same Eighty-Sixth Street block as my home building and the Bentley School. My teacher at the S.A.J., Judith Eisenstein, had the first bat mitzvah in New York; I followed her example.

Judith's father was Mordecai Kaplan, a rabbi who provoked argument when he revised the Hebrew prayer book, removing diminishing references to women and to other faiths, omitting "the chosen." At thirteen, summoned to the altar, I climbed creaky steps alone, gazed at my parents, grandparents, and E. McKnight Kauffer standing tall and lanky in a prayer shawl— and I proceeded to forget my text. The occasion weighed heavily on my shoulders. Wearing the taffeta dress my mother had picked out for me, hoping it didn't rustle too audibly, I felt inadequate to represent the judge Deborah or the heroic Judith of my Bible classes. I stumbled through my haftorah, mispronouncing the Hebrew, and for weeks afterward my proud grandfather would boast to befuddled bus drivers, construction workers, and waiters, "She used the Sephardic pronunciation."

Nervousness notwithstanding, the bat mitzvah was a ceremony I wanted. Since childhood I've identified with my father's sister, Helen, who rose through poverty to become a doctor in 1920s Warsaw. As a woman and a Jew, Helen was ordered to stand behind the back row during lectures in her university's amphitheater. Yet she earned her degree, trained, and treated patients. Even after the Nazi invasion of Poland, Helen believed her country would protect her, though she was a Jew, and that she would be allowed to treat her patients. In 1940, long after her parents had fled to safety in Palestine, she was confined to the Warsaw Ghetto and faced with the certainty of slaughter in a concentration camp. In a rage at the

Poles for giving her to the Nazis, Helen climbed a municipal tower, pulled down the Polish flag, wrapped it around her, and leaped, or was shot, to her death.

I was struck by Helen's photograph on our piano, her smile compassionate but icy, her prim, black, lace-trimmed dress cut unexpectedly low. Like women I had seen in a movie about Ivan the Terrible, she had high cheekbones and wide-set eyes that looked trusting and, at the same time, sharply inquisitive. I remembered my father's saying that Helen had introduced him to the poems of Adam Mickiewicz, which he read to me in Polish at bedtime. While I did not understand the words, I heard a clarinet's low register in his rough, emotive, declamatory strains that woke me to poetry. A child of my time and place, I wanted to transform the sorrow of Helen's death by reading and writing in English accents and rhythms learned from John Donne, George Herbert, and especially from Gerard Manley Hopkins, as in his "Carrion Comfort":

Mine, O thou Lord of life, send my roots rain.

Nevertheless, I grew into myself when I wrote in the voice of a Jew named Helen. She declined to walk, naked, to her death. The indignity of a concentration camp was a price she could not pay, not even for the hope of staying alive. To me, her act was iconic, drawing the imagination to it. Her very freedom had forced her to climb the steps of that tower, as though passivity had become repellent to her. For Helen, life was a series of committed choices.

Moore, Judith, Helen. Choice was what made them free. It is, in Sartre's terms, a dreadful freedom. Not circumstance, not luck, not even *what* it may be, but choice itself would shape

54

my days and tell me who I am.

My Hebrew background was of little comfort in difficult
times. To be sure, my bat mitzvah at thirteen and confirma-
tion at fourteen led to an attachment to Judaism that continued through my college years and beyond. I traveled to Israel
during my second summer at college and stayed in a kibbutz.
I celebrated Passovers with my parents, moved by songs in the
Haggadah. Still, Judaism offered me no answers, and perhaps
that's the point: the religion I came to know deepened my
faith—not in a mercurial, turbulent God, but in art. My persistent holy image was of King David dancing before the Ark
of the Covenant with all his might, shouting and playing the
harp in unison with trumpeters. In my mind he played a solo,
majestic and flowing. What a clamor there must have been!

My faith was in Sartre, who proclaimed responsibility for
individual acts. It was in the head-turning precision of a seemingly casual line in a drawing by Matisse. And higher still, it
was in Sonny Rollins playing serene blues on tenor saxophone.
Saint Ignatius of Loyola's "composition of place" informed my
poems. Once, I consulted a rabbi at Central Synagogue about
my roving affinities. Were they defections from Judaism? I
asked. "No," he said, after a pause. "I hope not. My son is a
medievalist who writes about *The Cloud of Unknowing*." In a
crafty move, whether or not intentional, the rabbi escorted me
from his study to the vast synagogue sanctuary, walked me to
the sacred *bimah*, a platform with an elegant wood-and-silver
door of the holy Ark, and began reciting a declaration of faith:
Shema yisroel adonai eloheinu adonai echod. Hear Israel, the
Lord our God, the Lord is one. Midway through the prayer, I

joined him. I had an answer to my questions of attachment.

If my faith was complicated, Jerry's was more so. Born a Jew, of a family not quite Orthodox but more observant than mine, he was a dutiful son and a quick study for his bar mitzvah. Later, though, he came to shun places of worship, winced at words like "soul," and shrank before the metaphysical. Science was his truth, empirical evidence his mainstay. Once I told him a story about Bertrand Russell, also a nonbeliever: a friend asked him what, when he went to heaven—as surely he would go to heaven—would he say to God when questioned why he did not believe. Russell answered, "You didn't give me enough evidence." I asked Jerry if that would be his answer to the Highest Judge. Jerry replied, "No, not *enough* evidence. I'll say 'You didn't give me *any* evidence.'"

Yet his actions spoke otherwise. He caught every performance he could of Bach's B Minor Mass, moved, he told me, by Bach's own belief in God. But it went further. I remember Jerry driving on the Hudson River Palisades with me and a friend, a renegade Catholic novelist named Arthur Roth. We were to visit Arthur's friend, a writer who was about to take orders as a priest. In a car that swerved along the steep cliffs, Jerry and Arthur talked of disbelief. Arriving at Maryknoll, we met Bill Flanagan, the novice, in a small, bare room. He was a jovial man who frowned as he spoke, lowering his glance as though reining in eyes that wanted to look everywhere they could. During our conversation, he stared at Jerry, and finally said: "Your work must be like mine. It gets to be a drag if you don't believe in it." Yes, that was it. Jerry's work was his faith.

And faith persisted. When my father lay dying, Jerry gave him a last injection of penicillin ("We can't let him die of an infection") and ordered a last transfusion ("We can't let him die of blood loss"). After he had done all he could medically, he told me to pray. At our un-ceremonial Jewish wedding, one gesture gave him away: Jerry had refused a head covering, then, halfway down the aisle, this atheist pulled a yarmulke out of his pocket and clapped it on his head. "For my father," he insisted, but I guessed the impulse lay deeper than that, in custom if not belief. And it persisted: at my mother's funeral, he was the first to shovel earth, the spade upside down.

For me, Jerry was Dr. Larivière in Flaubert's *Madame Bovary*, whose hands "were ungloved so as to touch suffering," and who was said to "practice virtue without believing in it." Flaubert brings in Dr. Larivière at the end of the novel, where the wise doctor tersely dismisses the ignorant bungling of the town hypocrites. For Jerry, belief in empiricism superseded religious faith, and yet his dedication to saving lives was, in a word, sacred.

6

THE LONG-LEGGED FLY

In 1961 we moved to a larger apartment in the same building, a one-bedroom. Even before we had a proper bed, Jerry constructed a sound system with a tuner, amplifier, and speakers, and a turntable that would play the Bach and Vivaldi record we bought on one of our first dates. After that came more furnishings, such as a hand-me-down mahogany dining table and chairs, gifts from both our parents. In both dark rooms I pasted Japanese rice paper on the windows, blocking out a dingy courtyard view, and hung lights on the ceiling.

Our first visitor was the nun I'd met in my medieval drama class who wore a floor-length black habit with a veil that kept getting caught in the crowded school elevator. She wanted to attend a lecture but could not return late to her New Jersey convent. As Jerry and I were on our way to dinner at a bistro, we saw her fly crow-like down the street. When she loomed before him, Jerry invited her to stay the night and gave her the key. I could see him swell to offer a new guest our new

sofa in our new living room. When we returned, Jerry opened
his closet door and found, on a hook, her veil slung over his
pajamas, their blue legs dangling under billowing black cloth.
In practical terms, it was the best place for the starched headdress, but it looked odd. We laughed, talked of our evenings,
and, before we retired, she blessed us and our marriage and
our habitat. Our new home was sanctified.

There was Marianne Moore, who came bringing us her
Collected Poems, which had just come out. In our apartment,
the object that caught her eye was a miniature landscape by a
young, little-known painter named David Vereano, who subsequently died of AIDS. What strikes me now, years later, is that
I wish I could have told him of her admiration.

Though we lived only a few blocks away from her apartment on West Ninth Street, she sent us letters frequently. She'd
begin with, "Dear Grace and Dr. Schulman," just as she started
letters to my parents with "Dear Marcella and Mr. Waldman."
We never understood the reason for that restraint, but sur-
mised it had to do with etiquette. One day, the "Dr. Schulman"
fell away. On November 19, 1961, we suddenly remembered it
was her birthday, and hastily wrapped and delivered a lavender scarf by Yves Saint Laurent that my father had given me.
Though elegant, the scarf had been one of the leftover presents
he'd ordered for his clients. We said nothing when Marianne
exclaimed, "How extravagant of you." But then she sent us a
note headed simply, "Dear Grace and Jerry," and we winced at
her teasing sentence: "You are not hoarders, I see." Of course,
she knew what we'd done, because my father had given her
one of the same surplus scarves.

I'd read her early correspondence with Ezra Pound, and

remembered his criticism of her image of a leopard "spotted underneath and on its toes." She'd replied, "Leopards are not spotted underneath, but in old illuminations they are, and on old Indian muslins, and I liked the idea that they are." Once when Jerry and I visited London, I found a postcard of a tapestry with—indeed!—a leopard spotted everywhere. I couldn't wait to bring it to Miss Moore. She'd had a stroke and was lying in bed, her white hair streaming over the pillow. "Here it is," I said. "Leopards spotted everywhere." She scrutinized the photograph, sat bolt upright in bed, and exclaimed, "Those are cheetahs, Grace!" and lay down again.

A powerful force in the early years of our marriage was our friendship with the novelist Richard Yates. It began in 1961 when I read the galleys of his first book, *Revolutionary Road*, and lost no time in arranging an interview for *Glamour*. It would appear among conversations with Marlon Brando and the tenor Franco Corelli. He nearly canceled the shoot when a photographer, who said he'd worked with Truman Capote, asked Dick to wear a turtleneck sweater, "as a writer should." Obviously he had the wrong writer. When we hired a more tactful photographer, Duane Michals, instead, Dick appeared, smiling, with searching gray eyes, looking elegant in a Brooks Brothers tweed jacket, oxford shirt, gray flannel trousers, and a red-and-blue striped tie. He walked in desert boots and carried an English trench coat. It was the only outfit he had.

We met on the coldest night of 1961. After the session with Duane Michals, he and I trudged downtown in a snowstorm and ducked into the Cedar Tavern, across University Place from our building. As we talked, a mutual attraction came on, and I stopped it short by saying, "Come over to the house and meet my husband." After a silent moment, we crossed a sludge-laden street to our home.

Thereafter Dick, Jerry, and I became inseparable. I was struck by the resemblance between the two men: both tall, fair, and lanky, with aquiline profiles. Both are what I thought, from his writing, F. Scott Fitzgerald should have looked like, and probably didn't. When Dick complained that his book jacket made him look too effeminate—"not ballsy enough," in his words—I took his picture on our roof against a red brick background. "Look ballsy, Dick," I said, and he clenched his teeth. My camera was but a simple model, but the photo became his trademark.

Evenings, the three of us would devour a pot of beef bourguignon, one of my easier dishes, while we talked about medicine and rated new novels, not an unlikely combination in our household. We were lifted by one another's presences, our conversations ablaze.

Dick had been recently divorced, and, since his separation, would bring his two daughters, Sharon and Monica, on weekends from their mother in Mahopac, New York, to his run-down, one-room basement apartment on Seventh Avenue South, in Manhattan. Sharon, at twelve, would act as four-year-old Monica's guardian. Jerry and I invited the three to stay in our apartment for their visit. Though small, it was preferable to Dick's studio. The girls would bring us the closest we ever came to raising children of our own. We five walked through Central Park, Monica riding high on Dick's shoulders, Sharon and I occasionally disappearing to rent bikes and wheel away. At the aquarium we nicknamed Monica "clownfish" and

Sharon "sea anemone."

I watched Jerry's fatherly inclinations blossom forth. He guided Sharon by advising her on high school and college. At home, while Sharon and I would prepare dinner, he'd mimic animals for Monica, or let her play with his stethoscope.

From the age of four, Monica was told that Jerry worked in a "mouse hospital," and assumed that he treated sick mice. When she asked to visit him at work, Jerry became nervous. He told her the truth, carefully, patiently, that he had to infect mice to keep little girls from getting sick. At the news, Monica cried nonstop. Years later, Jerry told her that he understood she cried because she'd been fooled. "No, because of those poor mice," she said. Later, the grown-up Monica was to confide that when she and Sharon married Jewish men, and Monica a Jewish doctor, Jerry, she said, had been their model.

We'd never had a friend like Dick. At one extreme he required high maintenance: an emotional imbalance led to irresponsible behavior, which Jerry had to curb with tact. At another extreme, Dick was morally incorruptible, with an aim for ethical perfection. He thought it detracted from one's own self-esteem to be harshly critical of others without their knowledge. Visiting us one evening, he picked up a glass beaker Jerry had brought home from his lab. Dick turned it into a bank, and insisted we feed it dimes whenever any of us lambasted absent people. The beaker was labeled "The Physicians and Authors' Benefit Fund" (PABF), whose proceeds would send a writer to medical school or a physician to a creative writing program. "Now that's finable," Dick would say, when the talk turned catty. "Yes, it's self-congratulatory, and that's costly," Jerry would agree. Dick's remarks were often finable for he did not suffer gladly the self-congratulation found in the 1960s, and would call the practitioners of mutual admiration "a circle jerk." One night when a bad but prize-winning novelist's name came up, Dick sprang to his feet, emptied his pocket of change, and only then let loose a stream of invective. That was the platonic Richard Yates, the man ever trying to define what was right, and to live up to his ideals. The dark Richard we didn't know until much later.

Dick and Jerry both adhered to standards, whether ethical or aesthetic. In books, Dick's faithful Penelope was Flaubert, with *Madame Bovary* his ideal achievement. He'd modeled *Revolutionary Road's* April Wheeler and her tragic fall on Emma Bovary's tragic decline. He said, "Both are provincial housewives who have love affairs. When Emma Bovary dies, I die." Although he was a major stylist, he suspected some writers of seducing with prose, and looked beyond style to structure. His preference was the classical curve of action, the unknowing character. *Billy Budd* was better than *Moby-Dick* because the latter sprawled. *The Great Gatsby*, shaped into a tragic fall, was better than *Tender Is the Night*. His canon comprised, after *Bovary*, Conrad's *Heart of Darkness*, Ford Madox Ford's *The Good Soldier*, Salinger's *The Catcher in the Rye*, Jane Austen's *Persuasion*, and, surprisingly, James Joyce's *Ulysses* ("I stretched my brain for it"), though *Finnegans Wake* "went beyond my comprehension."

Both men hated pretension. In college, I had been a *Mademoiselle* guest editor, along with ten other College Board winners, and we were called to New York in June 1952 to write the magazine's August issue. I worked with Cyrilly Abels, the managing editor, a fragile brunette who dressed smartly in designer suits with yellow chammy-leather gloves. Cyrilly had the foresight to publish long works by the likes of Faulkner, Dylan Thomas, Katherine Anne Porter, Flannery O'Connor, and James Baldwin, some for the first time nationally.

Now a literary agent, Cyrilly visited us with her husband, Jerome Weinstein. She adored him, though her friends rankled at his lengthy monologues, sometimes shouting, usually irrelevant. He seemed to crave the dominant role, as though abashed by Cyrilly's accomplishment. Once again, I was grateful that Jerry supported my writing, and enjoyed, as he said, my conviviality with others.

To me it seemed natural that Cyrilly should speak of the authors she knew, even by their first names: "Sir Charles" for C. P. Snow, "Frank" for O'Connor, "Carson" for McCullers, "Tennessee" with a notable absence of "Williams." Jerry said jokingly that she was the only woman in the world who could say "Churchill and Truman" in one sentence and mean Capote. And in a letter Dick was to write, he said: "Best regards to Cyrilly, C. P., Truman, Carson, Alfred, Guvvie, Frank, Ken, and the gang, and do thank them all for being so patient with her Jerome (dime enclosed)."

One summer, at the Bread Loaf Writers' Conference, Dick became wildly manic, berated others on the faculty, and was hospitalized involuntarily, diagnosed as manic psychotic. He was treated with drugs, but their effect was temporary. Back in New York, he continued his insulting behavior. A chain-smoker, he flicked his ashes dangerously near Cyrilly's lap, and, in a foggy voice, said, "You love them all, I know." He lost control, let loose a stream of curses entirely opposite to his usual care with language, put his head down on a mahogany table, and went to sleep.

Usually Dick was ultra-sane in his rightness, and deeply sympathetic. When he felt the madness coming on, he would drink steadily to avoid it. Correctness vanished. Rightness went awry. After he sold his apartment to teach at the Iowa Writers' Workshop, he would stay on our living room sofa during visits to New York. Once, late at night, Jerry away on a science visit, I heard the screech of boards and glass coming from the other room. Dick was thumping a glass table, shouting curses to imagined others, and, I thought, was a danger to himself. Looking at our friend, I saw him in opposite ways: uncontrolled and yet dazzling with rectitude, disordered and yet elegant, true. "Mental illness is no excuse for bad behavior," I heard myself say, turning sharply enough to snap my ponytail in the air. It worked, at least on that night.

Estrangement was foreordained, although we never stopped loving Richard Yates. He had awakened us both to hard aims whose results would be, for all we knew, permanent. Ten years after we first met, he wrote: "Knowing you both was one of the very few things that kept me sane during those drastic, dismal years of my second bachelorhood. I know I was an exasperating friend at times, but I can't ever thank you enough, or repay you, for the unflagging moral support you gave me when I needed it most. Don't ever forget that, either of you." That admission came from a noble man.

Even before I knew Dick's dark side, I was relieved that I hadn't married a literary man. Dick was adamant about his choices in books, and while I learned from his sensibilities, I wanted space to try my own. "You hear a different music,"

Jerry told me, and he was right. I had apprenticed myself to
the great poets, Catullus, Shakespeare, Hopkins, Donne. My
Crane was Hart, not Stephen. For a while I hesitated before
showing Dick my poems, especially after his pronouncement,
"Bad poems get by me, but the good never do." A reasonable
position, but occasionally he would contradict it: "Good poems
get by me, but the bad never do." When I finally did show
my work, he was diffident at first—he wished I'd worked
in prose—but finally enthusiastic. He advised me to leave
my job at *Glamour* and write. "Write with balls, Grace," he
commanded, and when I objected to the gender distinction he
replied, "Well, write with ovaries, Grace. Same thing." In his
estimation, Jane Austen had balls, and Katherine Mansfield
didn't. Gina Berriault had balls to spare, he insisted, adding
that she bested him and other male writers in an anthology
of *Esquire* fiction. Dick's principles were inflexible. His fierce
passion resulted in his delivery of sentences with exclamation
marks.

I could tell Jerry, but not Dick, that my major love was
William Butler Yeats, who, as far as I knew, had escaped Dick's
scrutiny. I'd found in Yeats's early poems an obsession with
folk ballads much like my own—"Ich am of Irlaunde" ring-
ing in my ears—and, in his later work, "The Circus Animals'
Desertion," a profound affirmation of self:

> I must lie down where all the ladders start
> In the foul rag and bone shop of the heart.

After some hesitation I quoted those lines to Dick, antici-
pating that the lying down to shed all masks might be considered a misadventure. The lines skirted dangerously one of his

precepts, that honesty per se is never a virtue in poetry or in prose fiction. Often Dick quoted Anatole France about the dog masturbating on your leg: "Sure it's honest, but who needs it?" Still, I had to praise those lines, adding my admiration for the personal, direct exclamatory address, such as Donne's "Death, be not proud," and Cavafy's "Body, remember." To my surprise, Dick understood.

Like Dick, Jerry had been after me to leave *Glamour* to write, insisting that our savings could cover at least two years without my salary. He'd been annoyed when the editors ran a makeover story about me, a before-and-after feature with extensive photographs by Gordon Parks. He was appalled when he saw pictures of me playing the guitar in a designer silk shirt and velvet pants, painted with heavy makeup and fake lashes.

I did take their advice and left *Glamour* in 1962, after two years, but only after some revelations led me to it. First, Jerry and I went to hear Thelonious Monk play at a bar near Astor Place. Monk stabbed notes as though they were hot pans, heels dug into the wooden stage, soles flapping like seals. Suddenly he snapped his fingers, as though to shape pain into order. I realized then that this was form, the shaping out of darkness, as in Creation, not the smoothness of line I was taught to provide at the magazine. I wanted to make art, not copy.

Second, I was assigned to write an article about correct bodily posture, and Jerry referred me to an expert who studied the spine in a "gait laboratory" at New York Hospital. In the course of our interview, he told me that wearing high heels was wrong for good posture. When I wrote the story, *Glamour*'s shoe editor killed it, cursing, with a reprimand. "No, I won't have you censored by a shoe editor," Jerry announced that evening.

The third, and final, blow came when I was asked to find a poem for a photographic spread of women on the beach. I wrote one, juvenilia, but mine. The magazine editor said fine, and proceeded to remove my signature. "Your poem is our editorial statement," she said. My identity endangered, I left the job.

Good fortune arrived in a psychoanalyst Jerry phoned who referred me to another competent professional. Earlier attempts at therapy had been bungled. In excited moments I'd seen common things—a sketch on the wall, a vase of dahlias—moving when they were still. One therapist I'd been sent to early in my adolescence had told me and my parents that my delusional episodes were a sure sign of schizophrenia. I'd lived weighted by that diagnosis, and in time I felt safe only with a normative structure, such as a nine-to-five job. The new psychoanalyst pointed out finally that in this case passion could cause the rapid heartbeat, the visual distortion, and encouraged me to stand by my illusions. Suddenly I had a new respect for the power of feelings, no longer content to repress them for propriety. The revelation fortified me to stay home and write.

My wardrobe changed. I put aside the blonde, brushed-mohair suit with the tight skirt I'd hobbled in at *Glamour* for a simple white shirt and cotton overalls. I walked through Washington Square Park, stepping warily to avoid a man, probably a writer out of work, whose sole occupation seemed to be picking up women. I stared at a leafless chestnut tree, its trunk gnarled with blight. The branches trembled. I shook with fear. What if the absence of conventional routine were to threaten my emotional balance? Dick's psychosis came to mind.

Then my fear turned to exhilaration: sparrows were flying at
the branches, making them *seem* to move. I thought of Veronica,
the pallid saint coming alive with the imprint of Christ's face
on her veil. So, too, the birds imprinted that tree, animating it,
bringing it to life. It was a metaphor—or, perhaps, a miracle.

Those sparrows flew into an early poem, "Birds on a Blighted
Tree," pressing their Veronicas on it, and gave me the lines,
"Free things breed freedom; / That dead arm beating."

Dancing the sardana on my pre-wedding excursion to
Barcelona led to:

> Strangers we stand alone but turn together
> as vanes become a windmill in the wind;
> one hand opens for another hand,
> the wheel breaks only to include another.

How joyful it was to serve language, to listen for the music
of the line, for words and for the silences between them. At the
same time, and despite Jerry's unhesitant support, I couldn't get
used to financial dependence. And besides, I couldn't write all
the time. Having started an MA at Johns Hopkins while working as a news reporter, I knew that I wanted to teach poetry.

When I enrolled in graduate courses at N.Y.U., the effect
was surprising. Suddenly I became a good student after getting
lower than As, first as a sidetracked high-school pupil and later
as a lost undergraduate. She was buried and gone, the eighteen-
year-old who spent sleepless nights struggling futilely with
assignments. My graduate work at N.Y.U. became more than a
vocational means to an end. Whether it was by metamorphosis,
alchemical change, or simply focus, and strange as it may be, I

couldn't get enough of it.

Unlike the creative-writing program that was to flourish in that university, the PhD in literature that I knew demanded a six-period oral examination following coursework and preceding a dissertation. When I told Dick that the work would shape my writing hours and lead eventually to a livelihood, he scoffed at first, expressing his fear that I'd become "just another fucking PhD." He softened later, saying, "Well, it sure beats the hell out of writing for *Glamour* magazine." Dick's view notwithstanding, graduate study was alive. I read Henry James with a professor who walked with me in Washington Square Park to name the writer's favorite trees. I studied Anglo-Saxon poetry with Jesse Bessinger, who in classes played a harp he'd bought at the British Museum, a replica of one found in a king's burial ship at England's Sutton Hoo. I felt close to the mysterious speakers of Anglo-Saxon poems, to Cædmon and Deor and to the suffering woman of "The Wife's Lament." Their voices wandered into my own poems. Whitby Abbey intrigued me, the seventh-century double monastery for men and women set in England's moors. It was headed by—imagine!—a woman, Hild, who overheard the song of Cædmon, our first English poet. I wrote of it in "The Abbess of Whitby," and intended to major in the Anglo-Saxon period. Then one day, walking in a hall between classes, I heard the voice of someone reading my own William Butler Yeats:

> *Like a long-legged fly upon the stream*
> *His mind moves upon silence,*

The voice caught the poet's sensibility. I thought of Jerry's silences, and of how the words had entered my life and understood my marriage. The voice reading Yeats belonged to M. L. ("Mack") Rosenthal, a poet and critic. That day I changed my major to modern poetry. Rosenthal would become my Virgil and guide me through the process. When I told Marianne Moore about my plan, she was skeptical at first. "I never got a PhD, and T. S. Eliot never got a PhD, and Ezra Pound never did. And yet you persist. How is your *work*?" But when I asked to tape-record conversations with her toward a dissertation on her poetry, she said, "Well, if this is *about* me, I should participate." The dissertation would appear as a book, *Marianne Moore: The Poetry of Engagement*. And years later I would edit a complete edition of her poems, restoring those she omitted from her last volume, though she curiously called it "complete."

Though my work never emulated her style, I learned about writing from her. Urgency, economy, observation, curiosity. And most of all, joy. They were her watchwords. I was apprenticed to a master.

I was on my way. Then came the fatal call.

7

THE CRASH

One night in 1964 the doorbell rang. Raphael "Ray" Rudnik appeared, asking if we wanted to have a cheeseburger and fries at Steak and Brew. His proposal, seemingly ordinary, surprised us. Ray was a poet who was given to extrasensory beliefs that Jerry disparaged. Minutes before he rang, Jerry had said, "Let's call Ray and have a cheeseburger and fries at Steak and Brew." In the hilarious dinner conversation that followed, we never mentioned the coincidence.

We returned home, laughing, with Ray. Suddenly a phone call slashed the merriment. It came from Jerry's brother, Edward. Their parents had been in a head-on collision, while on the way to visit Edward's family in Boston. Meyer, their seventy-year-old father, the driver, had crossed the highway divider—he had no memory of how or why—and crashed into an oncoming car, killing an elderly man and injuring his grown children. Their mother, Shirley, suffered broken bones. The four survivors were being treated in a small hospital's emergency room on the road near Edward's family home.

Ray looked at me, pained, and left. Jerry and I made for the Austin-Healey and drove to the hospital, where we found his mother dying and his father badly hurt. While Jerry reached for their hospital charts, I stared at the watch on his father's wrist, its face cracked and stained with blood. Jerry and his brother spoke in medical language I didn't understand.

"Please explain," I asked.

"If only there were a pattern," Jerry said. "It changes from hour to hour."

That night Jerry and I stayed in a motel nearby, neither of us speaking at dinner. Jerry was dazed with the task to come. He and his brother were to superintend the care not only of their parents but also of the injured victims.

When we returned to New York, we learned by phone that their mother was dead. His father was released from the hospital, his fractured thigh bone never to heal properly, his spirit cracked. Months later, Jerry drove him to a Massachusetts courtroom where he was tried for vehicular homicide. Although he was acquitted, and remarried less than a year after ("for survival," he told his sons and watched their pained expressions), he remained haunted for the rest of his life.

Nor did Jerry and I recover easily from the tragedy. I'd been scheduled to take my comprehensive written examination one week after the crash. Thinking of Audrey Hepburn, who, in *The Nun's Story*, plays a sister faced with a choice to help another holy woman by failing an exam, I prayed: "Save my mother-in-law and I'll fail." On every line of the test paper I saw Shirley's handwriting. I failed, miserably, and by rule of law, was permitted to a six-period oral examination.

The oral was more rigorous. In the committee room, flanked by six male professors, I went dumb. Again I failed. Permitted to take it again in one year, I passed "with distinction." I owe that honor to Mack Rosenthal, who jocularly asked me, when I entered that hellish interrogation room, "Grace, who wrote *Hamlet*?" After that, I relaxed, smiled, and navigated through the six periods, from *Beowulf* through Ezra Pound. From then on, I would write what I loved—even though they called it a dissertation—all the way through the PhD. I was home free.

After the accident, Jerry was never the same. "Ed—she wanted Ed—until the last. It was—Ed—all the time," he said when the phone call came, sobbing, in a stammer that began only at that moment and lasted for years. He enrolled as a patient in a clinic run by the New York State Psychiatric Institute, where famous doctors treated select candidates for whatever they could afford. After the first few sessions, his psychoanalyst was mugged, clubbed over the head, and killed on a well-lighted side street in the East Eighties, on his way home from a concert at the Y.

Following a week spent mourning for Shirley, Jerry went on with his work, fulfilled obligations, and managed the role of a devoted husband. For his father and stepmother, we did what we could. We attended their wedding, fast as it was after Shirley's death, and saw him settled in a new life. But Jerry spoke less, and never a word about the tragedy. With the absence of talk about sensitive things, the tensions became fissures in our marriage that remained unsealed.

8

THE MYSTERY OF MARRIAGE

Despite the silences, we grew closer. My poems came pouring out. Jerry read my work and made cogent, candid comments, then attended all of my readings without minding the repetitions. When discouraged, I turned to him for assurance. One day, trashing more than one hundred drafts made painstakingly on my standard Remington typewriter, I cried out in desperation, "I'm no writer!" Calmly he responded, "No, you're an actor: act like you can write." His retort stays with me, even as I write these sentences, along with Kafka's "Warten" ("Wait") and Samuel Beckett's "Fail better."

Jerry was more certain of what he wanted to be his contribution to influenza virus research. Through him I learned that influenza, seemingly prosaic, was a mass murderer, killing millions globally. I delved into his papers, less savvy about his words than he was about mine, but nevertheless struck by his determination to increase resistance to infection and reduce the spread.

I was especially drawn to one of his papers written in 1969. The title daunted me at first: "The Role of Antineuraminidase Antibody in Immunity to Influenza Virus Infection."* But I read on and lost my initial reserve. His writing alone—strong verbs, compression—whetted my interest, despite my limited knowledge. The finding in the paper, along with work he did with Dr. Peter Palese, would become the basis of a new vaccine approach that is still being developed and of FDA-approved drugs such as Tamiflu.

Impressively, Jerry didn't fight to be the earliest to reveal information. Indeed, he declined to claim ownership, or even identity, believing that scientific discoveries belonged not to the doers but to a universal fund of knowledge. More than once I'd hear one of his colleagues vie for credit, and I was proud that Jerry never did.

After work, we talked. At sundown, as we sat drinking homemade daiquiris on our building's roof, high above the noise of traffic sirens, I warmed to his army stories I'd heard before. There was the one where his commanding officer had asked him to check the local water supply because a few cases of typhus had been reported in the area. "You don't get typhus from water. You may be thinking of typhoid fever," Jerry said, "and that will take some investigation."

"Typhus, typhoid, it's the same thing. Check the water!" the officer shouted. Jerry said he went back to barracks and returned a few hours later. "Nobody will get typhus from that water," he attested, before examining the typhus patients.

---

*Jerome L. Schulman, M.D. "The Role of Antineuraminidase Antibody in Immunity of Influenza Virus Infection." *Bulletin of the World Health Organization* (Bulletin de Organisation mondiale en Santé), 41 (1969), 647-65

Our faces glowed as we watched the sun redden rows of
Greenwich Village houses, and saw the walkers diminish on
the streets below us. Yes, there were minor squabbles—on
evenings together, why couldn't I wait for him before bound-
ing out of the house; why didn't I call when I came home late;
why did I, not he, have to be the heavy when arguing with
the landlord—but on our building's lofty roof, those quarrels
disappeared.

Jerry was eager to do more than his share of household
chores, unusual for his generation. His specialty was steaks
broiled with herbs, and on one Thanksgiving, a roasted goose.
Clumsily I dropped the bird when taking it from the oven,
and it went sailing across the floor, past my seated parents.
Restored, brushed off, it made a fine dinner, but I avoided
Jerry's frown.

My parents had pooled the housework, too, and I was used
to my father's complaints that his wife's bed-making did not
live up to his specifications. Jerry's gripe was that I sent towels
to the laundry rather than spin them in our basement machine.
"They're our tow-wels," I heard him mutter, in annoyance.
That, too, we survived.

We walked through the Metropolitan Museum galleries on
Friday evenings, when the crowds dispersed. Once we gazed in
wonder at portraits of George Washington, and talked of how
we, both descendants of immigrants, were moved by our first
president and by America's beginnings. On vacations we went
to the ocean, to Jerry's delight. In Manhattan Beach, he had
frolicked in the waves every day with his father and brother.
I, too, remember hankering for the shore in my native
Brooklyn, though it was never an everyday reality as I'd not

been taken there.

With friends, Jerry and I rented a share in a Fire Island house, which cost us three hundred dollars for a long summer. Crowded it was, and living with a dozen people was never easy. It was usual to hear such accusations as "Where's my toothpaste?" or "I just swabbed the countertop, and look at it now!" We cooked by kerosene lamps in the absence of electricity, or broiled on the deck grill, and pulled wagons to the ferry that carried our food. Since there were no cars and no roads, we traveled barefoot on sand. And there was beauty. When sunset inflamed both sides of the narrow sand strip, Jerry strode down to the water and plowed through the waves, in that light a stick figure in foamy tiers, waving a careless hand.

Every winter we went for a week to find low-priced hotels in the Caribbean. At an inn in Martinique, Auberge de l'Anse Mitan, French families conversed across separate tables. We made friends with a businessman from Paris, who took us with his family to Mount Pelée, a dormant volcano. In Nevis, Jerry and I swam in water so clear I could see our legs shimmering in streaks of light. On that small island, where the Caribbean Sea meets the Atlantic Ocean, I saw divisions everywhere: the sun rose over whitecaps in in a volatile ocean and set over a calm sea; life coursed in the blood-red bougainvillea and death loomed in the palm fronds that waved like clock hands and in the fish bones that stalked the coast. I was constantly reminded of the slaves drowned in the middle passage. There we dived and snorkeled in waves so powerful that a breakwater was built to keep them back, a miles-long row of giant's teeth. We climbed jetties and walked through gardens of trumpet flowers and ixoras, always hearing the ocean's drumroll. Nights we heard cadenzas of sonorous roars that lulled us to sleep.

Summers awakened the urge to walk, or more likely to run, in Europe, seldom planning an itinerary in advance for the surprise of new places. There was the time we boarded a train from Barcelona heading we didn't know where and got off when we saw mountains of sand sloping off to the sea. And Paris, always Paris. We made it ours by ignoring the sternness of concierges, the off-handedness of waiters, the hauteur of passersby. We mocked the indifference and, forgetting ourselves, merged with it. We went from the airport to the Place Saint-Sulpice, where we lost no time in leaving our one bag at the compact, inexpensive Hôtel Récamier, and savored a sensual painting by Delacroix, *Jacob Wrestling with the Angel*, hanging at the late Gothic church of the square. Then, after sitting in a café, we retraced our footsteps from the wedding trip, following our younger selves down the Seine to gaze at Cézanne's *Bathers* and *The Card Players*. At night we hiked to Montmartre for a restaurant where diners at separate tables spontaneously broke out in a traditional drinking song, "Boire un petit coup c'est agréable." After a few choruses, we joined in.

Fast, but not superficial. On those trips we attained a heightened intensity. Not even in the drug-taking sixties did we need relaxants or stimulants to reach those peaks. And the highest was England. In London we stayed near Trafalgar Square, near bookshops and theaters with cheap prices. Prawn sandwiches before shows did nicely for dinners. We saw Shakespeare plays that featured "doubling," where the same actors played two characters: the fool and Cordelia in *King Lear*, Hermione and Perdita in *The Winter's Tale*. I thought of our "doubling." We were merging into two halves of one person. We spoke the same lines, thrilled to the same scenes. When one was onstage, the other was in the wings, watching. How long would this continue?

London was a city of books: many Underground passengers carried paperbacks, graffiti on a brick wall consisted of a line by Oscar Wilde, and sketches of Dickens hung in restaurants. We bought a literary guidebook to England, rented a car, and covered its landmarks. We stood by Henry James's Lamb House at Rye, with its high brick wall and paved courtyard, and drove up mountains to the Lake District of Wordsworth and Coleridge. For Jerry there was Thomas Hardy's Dorset, for me the poet-priest George Herbert's parish in Bemerton— though when we arrived and asked an innkeeper for directions, he said, "Herbert? He hasn't been around here lately."

My most startling discovery was the seventh-century Whitby Abbey. On its grounds stood Cædmon, our first poet, and Hild, the unlikely monastery boss who overheard the aged cowherd in a barn and thought an angel had commanded him to sing. The story had always been dreamlike for me, but the landscape was even more so. The Abbey stands on a moor, not far from the sea. Jerry waited in the car while I walked, lost my way in the lunar country, saw dizzying horizons revolve above me, heather-filled craters below. Then my eyes caught that death's head, Whitby Abbey, preserved but standing like a rotting skull, black seabirds shrieking through white-socketed eyes that once held windows.

I located Jerry in the car and told him what I now knew to be true. Cædmon had sung there. He had made a new music out of the fusion of scops bellowing warlike songs in English

In Washington Square Park, September 15, 1957.

As a reporter, at the ticker-tape machine in the newsroom of the *Alexandria Gazette*, 1953.

The Bentley School, 48 West Eighty-Sixth
Street, where Grace was enrolled from
the ninth grade through graduation. Her
family lived on the block at 20 West.

Grace's paternal aunt Dr. Helen Waldman-
Gold, who leaped or was shot from a tower
in the Warsaw Ghetto, 1943, the Polish flag
wrapped around her.

E. McKnight Kauffer in his New York studio, 1940s.

Wedding at the Plaza Hotel, September 6, 1959.

Marianne Moore (center) at the Schulman wedding, flanked by
wedding guests Marjorie and Ashley Montagu.

Teaching as a graduate assistant
at N.Y.U., October 25, 1967.

In 1964, on a friend's terrace
overlooking Central Park.

Jerry in Greece, September 1959. "In Hydra we looked death in the face.
Or was it life at its highest elevation?"

In Tossa del Mar, Spain, on an impromptu trip. "We boarded
a train from Barcelona heading we didn't know where."

(L) Jerry in Tossa del Mar. (R) Jerry in the Microbiology Laboratory, Mount Sinai. "Through him
I learned that influenza, seemingly prosaic, was a mass murderer, killing millions globally."

At Yaddo, 1973, front row, between poets Tomaž Šalamun and Carl Rakosi. Irene Kirk is
at the left of Šalamun. Jules Feiffer and Susan Crile are in the background.

With W. S. Merwin and Jorge Luis Borges in the Green Room
of the Poetry Center, 92nd Street Y.

Richard Yates on the roof of One
University Place, June 1, 1962

With Alfred Corn, in the Conservatory
Garden, Central Park.

(L) Springs, East Hampton. On "the beautiful headland that was unbeautifully named Louse Point."
(R) Dore Ashton and Matti Megged. "We scrambled on the Walking Dunes, a stretch of sand hills
inland . . . and told linked stories, one person picking up another's narrative."

(L) With Karl Kirchwey at the celebration for her Frost Medal for Distinguished Lifetime Achievement in American Poetry, April 21, 2016. (R) With Jerry at Harvey Shapiro's birthday party in Brooklyn. The figure in the back is Victor Navasky.

With Richard Howard at a celebration for his writing, 2017.

and monks chanting praise in Latin. And he instinctively reversed them, wisely choosing the heaven of the monks and the rock-hard sounds of a burgeoning English language for praise.

> *Nu sculon herigean heofonrices Weard,*
> Now we shall praise heaven's keeper

Hild made Cædmon a monk, for she recognized the miracle that had made him a poet.

Wherever we were, tensions pursued us. They flew faster than jet planes, blew through open train windows, came after us on our walks. Their source was infertility. Although our barrenness was verified in 1962, we couldn't speak of the situation fully until twenty years later. An accident at birth had caused Jerry's sterility, which was discovered in tests after we tried for pregnancy. Although his virility was unaffected by the count, the fact of zero sperm had stunned him more than I understood at the time.

In the absence of talk, angry quarrels started over an ambivalent desire to adopt a child. Ironically, although Jerry treated others wisely, he had little insight into his own condition or, indeed, into knowing whether he wished to adopt. I, too, was confused. Our lack of direct communication in the matter was almost, but not entirely, the fault of the repressive air of our upbringing. And worse, even in the early 1960s— before the sexual revolution with its "free love" banners—sex and procreation were spoken of in euphemisms or not at all. When we couldn't converse openly about sex, words rusted. Tight-lipped, we encountered other frictions as well. After I left *Glamour* to write, and before beginning a teaching career, I became dependent on Jerry's income, while wishing for my own. It seeped into our marriage like smoke, tolerable at first, clinging to the ceiling, gradually making it hard to breathe. We didn't know it was a signal for fire.

9

BOTH OF US TOGETHER,
EACH APART

Then came the great social changes of the late sixties, which Jerry and I celebrated together while, paradoxically, drifting farther apart. Let me explain. The folk songs we sang on the fountain's ledge in 1957, one of them pledging to "study war no more" were no match for the horrors in Vietnam, the protracted, costly, twenty-year war cursed by horrors like Lt. William Calley's My Lai massacre, or the heavy bombing of North Vietnam ordered by then-president Richard Nixon. Living in Greenwich Village in the late sixties, we witnessed anti-establishment protests of newer groups—from the peaceable hippies to the violent Weathermen—that replaced our hopeful folksingers.

Instead of singing for peace, I carried an anti-war picket with the students I taught as a graduate assistant at N.Y.U. Joan Baez was singing "What Have They Done to the Rain," addressing the dangers of nuclear testing in the atmosphere. Although our charismatic Pete Seeger was still active, overshadowing even the new Bob Dylan and the Beatles, he was singing a different tune. His song "We Shall Overcome" lost star billing to "God Bless the Grass," as Seeger's one-world fervor was matched by his desire to preserve the land.

In effect, Jerry and I neglected our guitars. I lauded the new liberations: the Civil Rights Act, the proposed Equal Rights Amendment. I discussed them in my classes and Jerry listened to the changing views of his medical students at Mount Sinai. Without slighting the curriculum, we favored the efforts of our students to examine and question those in power, not simply to accept what was expected of them. My N.Y.U. professor Robert Corrigan spoke out against blind obedience to authority and disrespect for women and the young. Corrigan, who taught dramatic literature and founded the Tisch School of the Arts, hired me as his research assistant. He and his wife, Elizabeth, a rock singer, became our friends. One night the four of us, at his instigation, went to a faculty Halloween party dressed as characters from *The Balcony*, Jean Genet's play set in a brothel. Playing the clients who enact illusions of power, Corrigan and Jerry wore academic robes, as the Bishop and the Judge, respectively. I wore a long black dress as the Queen, head of the brothel; and Elizabeth put on a flimsy gown as Chantal, one of the whores. As the evening wore on, we found ourselves improvising lines and speaking out, in a Genet-based satire: the Judge condemned another customer, the Bishop refused to forgive a sinner, and Chantal danced a snaky bossa nova. After mixed notices—some cheers, some glares— from a straitlaced faculty, we left for the Corrigans' house in Washington Mews.

One summer Corrigan sent me to work as an intern for

Joseph Papp at the New York Shakespeare Festival. My job, at the Delacorte Theater in Central Park, was to record changes in *Troilus and Cressida* by watching rehearsals and performances. For the scene of Troy burning, orange lights shone, emitting a glow suggesting ancient Trojan fires, but also the current Vietnam War. Night after night I watched Troy consumed in that hideous light. Remarkably, though, through the trees surrounding the open-air theater, I could watch my grandmother's home on East Eighty-Sixth Street, in the building I'd visited often as a child. Now it went up in red-yellow flame. Every night it burned down. After a week, reality and art were a blur in my mind. The experience proved to me the power of Shakespeare to move through time, showing three wars in three ages as one—the Greeks', his, and finally, mine.

While I balked at words such as "self-actualization" as being too general to be understood, I supported the principles. Jerry, too, applauded the new freedom. He shamed the Mount Sinai faculty into advancing a woman as a surgeon. He found black and Asian experts to lecture in his virology seminars. And to the detriment of our marriage, he ragged me—in retrospect, rightly—for accepting his dole beyond his two-year offer of financial support.

But I was cursed with the sign of promise, that notorious destroyer of complacency. I earned my PhD in a Cinderella-like transformation from the unnoticed to the recipient of an Andiron Award for "best dissertation," a study of Marianne Moore's art that would become a book. Then came the most ironic for this previously poor student, a Founders' Day Award with its unforgettably formidable phrasing: "in recognition of having achieved a place in the highest bracket of scholastic preferment recognized by the University."

Jerry, who was entrusted with opening my letters from magazines lest they be disappointing rejections, proudly announced my first acceptance in *Poetry* magazine. It was a poem that had to do with my first failed oral, called "The Examination: Remembrance of Words Lost." Other poetry acceptances followed.

And still I could not put my foot in the academic door. At job interviews I was asked whether my marriage would interfere, and did I intend to have children. When I expressed my salary needs to an English department chair we knew, he asked, to my humiliation, if Jerry needed money.

Rather than fight the social inequality, I blamed myself, and, to my cost, wrongly, the state of our marriage. That fault-finding increased our resentments, which grew into quarrels.

Sex was bad. I suspected he had been seeing another woman who phoned him at home, usually with a question about a suffocating asthma. I knew her, but when I tried to assist her, she asked for him. "I must comfort her," he said after one conversation, and left to do so. I was annoyed. We needed to talk, not flee into an easier relationship. But speech was difficult, understanding scant.

One desperate afternoon we heard in a church concert a Bach cantata that began, "My God, what horrors next." It expressed my thoughts. Jerry had just admonished me for sending towels to the commercial laundry rather than mastering the building's machines. That scolding was an evasion of bigger issues. We parted in 1971, a year that coincided with a lucky break in my career.

I cannot say how long the separation lasted, because we were together for much of it. A few weeks after it happened, Jerry attended my PhD ceremony together with my parents, and shared their pride. I was especially grateful they came because it was a "plain-clothes" graduation: I hadn't yet acquired a gown and the rented ones failed to arrive in time. I saw them from the platform, though, and it felt real. Afterward, at a restaurant, my mother presented me with a gold medal dangling from a pin which she'd found at an antiques shop on Second Avenue; Jerry gave me a blank, lined notebook, with a card reading "Fill it up." Noticing our affection for one another, they didn't believe we were split.

Although Jerry had moved into a one-room studio I found for him in Greenwich Village, on Perry Street, he came to our apartment often and still called it home. He stayed there when I flew to Ireland on a plane ticket my father gave me, having won it in a raffle at a business lunch on Saint Patrick's Day, with the holiday as its theme. I'd dreamed of leaving my footprints on James Joyce's beach, Sandymount Strand, where Stephen Daedalus resolved to devote his life to art. Once there I pocketed a black stone bisected by a white line, marveling at how so little in nature was that symmetrical. Walking across the Baggot Street Bridge, I stopped in Parsons Bookshop and found, to my surprise, a little pamphlet called a broadside with my name in bold letters on the outside, and my poem "Burn Down the Icons" printed inside. The bookseller put me in touch with the Seafront Press, whose publisher said they'd suddenly come upon funds to produce booklets of poems by, among others, Ann Lauterbach and Peter Straub. A schoolmate, Tom Dillon Redshaw, had sent them my poem when it

had appeared in the *American Poetry Review*, and they added it
to the series.

My new friends at Seafront Press escorted me to a pub that
hosted poetry readings, and we heard Austin Clarke read from
his book imprinted by Liam Miller's Dolmen Press in Ireland.
Dublin had an impersonal amiability that won me: one woman,
directing me to an address, blessed me with "God and Mary go
with you." A man, asked for directions to Trinity College, took
me there, reciting its history on the way. I wished that I could
stay longer, but returned home to get my life in order.

Once Jerry slept in the apartment for weeks when I was
giving poetry readings in London. One afternoon he took a
telephone message: a request for me to show up for a job
interview at Baruch College. Resolutely, he set a date, met my
plane at the airport, and took me there—but to a bar first, saying, "I have to talk down your London accent. You catch
it every time."

Beginning as an adjunct that autumn, I worked up through
the ranks. I loved teaching literature to urban students, many
of them hungry for the education their parents never had. They
seemed glad to have a poet reading the classics with them, and
the long winter and summer breaks allowed me time to write.
I relished the new independence. Some five years before, I had
been refused a credit card without my husband's authorization,
and now I was proud to have a bank account in my name. My
first paycheck at Baruch contained eight extra dollars, the sum
distributed to all women faculty at CUNY by a woman professor, the winner of a legal battle against discrimination. I never
met the woman identified only as Leyla, but her gift to me
spoke eloquently of the new equality. I smiled when I remem-

bered my forty-dollar paycheck fifteen years before, when I had been a news reporter on the *Alexandria Gazette*, earning ten dollars less each week than the male reporters.

Despite our marriage troubles, and they seemed to come in battalions, we stayed in love. We cheered each other's dreams. Jerry encouraged me throughout to write as well as I could. The rift marked a dramatic phase: Independence was mine. Freedom was mine. I gave up a heavy cigarette habit. I found friends, among them Naomi Lazard, the central character of Bill Knott's poetry collection *Nights of Naomi*. Once she agreed to visit my class as I taught the book, and she swept in, slim, curvy, and unsmiling, to the surprise of my undergraduates. Another was Brian Swann, a poet from Northumberland who translated Italian poetry and wrote about Native American literatures, believing that their mannerisms were akin to those of his native county. Brian asked me to be his witness when he applied for U.S. citizenship—and regretted it. When asked whether he belonged to any group that advocated anarchy, I cried out, "He doesn't have to answer that, on the First and Fifth Amendments!" He nudged me, saying, "Quiet, or you'll fuck up my naturalization." Summers, Brian and I traveled to the Karolyi Foundation in Vence, France, where artists lived and worked on a mountaintop in the Maritime Alps. When we returned from our last trip I threw an engagement party for him and his bride, Roberta.

Other bonds followed. Willard Trask, the renowned translator, taught me his own English versions of French and Italian songs of the Middle Ages. As a naturalist, he instructed the naming of Central Park trees, from lindens through elms to honey locusts. When he died in 1979, he left me his treasured *Oxford English Dictionary*, in microprint with a magnifying glass, and it became a talisman. Philip Schultz, whose poems I'd read even before we met at Yaddo, was all that a friend could be. We swapped poems, and our comments kept each other afloat. Once when Phil said he especially admired a long, ambitious poem I'd shown him, I said it had come back rejected by magazines I listed for him. He thought for a while before replying, "All those rejections? I didn't know it was *that* good a poem."

Those men were platonic friends, and they added to the relief I'd felt with Dick Yates that I hadn't married a writer. Still, my feelings for them taught me that distance could promote mutual respect. In contrast, Jerry and I had been close to a fault, sending out our needs to one another the way a grapevine sends out tendrils to cedar branches they destroy. My hours with Brian, and later with Phil, opened windows on a marriage that had needed air.

After a time of living alone, I had an affair that fell apart when I smiled in the midst of serious talk, thinking of Jerry's laughter. I had another, same ending. Jerry had one that lasted longer than my brief liaisons, but he came home to our apartment even while it raged on, and eventually he broke it off. I was glad by then to be child-free. In that same magical year of 1971, I began what was to be my thirty-six-year tenure as the *Nation*'s poetry editor.

The *Nation* won me. A surprise phone call came from James Storrow, then the publisher, who said he liked four of my poems in the current issue and would I consider being the new poetry editor. I looked at the phone, amazed. I had been writing in obscurity, my marriage was failing, and money was scarce. Before Baruch College I'd had no job at all. And why me, an unknown? Were there not better-known poets who deserved his trust? I soon discovered that it was the magazine's remarkable policy to take a chance on emerging writers, giving them complete editorial freedom to do their work. Usually those writers left within a few years for a higher opportunity, sometimes in a blaze of recognition. Little did Storrow suspect I would be editing the *Nation*'s poems for more than three decades.

Besides entrusting me with poetry, the *Nation* entertained my earlier affinity for journalism. Utilizing skills I'd picked up while working as a reporter on a small daily, I volunteered to read proof and help with layout design. In the beginning of my tenure, I went to the office more than I had to, engrossed with back issues in the archives. I marveled at the original board of 1865, which included William James and Henry James, Longfellow, William Cullen Bryant. I liked the magazine's continuing purpose, "for politics and the arts," and its intransigent insistence on a free press. I savored the last poems of Yeats and D. H. Lawrence, and I read articles by Henry James (blasting Whitman's *Drum-Taps*) and by Thomas Higginson (praising Emily Dickinson, referring to his earlier ambivalence about her work). Looking for minor figures, I was especially attracted to a nineteenth-century writer named Gail Hamilton, of Massachusetts, who wrote on a woman's right to remain single. History rose up from my desk, a splintery wooden table that might have been used by the likes of Henry James.

Submissions came in envelopes, unannounced, unheralded, and sometimes without introductory letters. All that mattered were the poems, addressed to the poetry editor of the *Nation* and accompanied by stamped, self-addressed envelopes, from little known poets to those I'd revered, and from places like Abilene, Kansas, to metropolitan cities. Early on, I received two poems from Mark Van Doren, a celebrated critic and former literary editor of the magazine. Staring at the postmark, I realized they'd been sent a day before he died: I pictured him sliding them into a metal box or driving them to the local post office, one of his last acts. And, thank the stars, they were good. Later on, I shivered at the beauty of two classics, dropped on my desk by a mail carrier who must not have known he was holding fire: James Wright's "Hotel Lenox" and "To a Blossoming Pear Tree."

James Storrow, amused by my attraction to the *Nation*'s past, took me to lunch and told me stories about his forebears, the Storrows of Boston, such as an aunt, the poet Amy Lowell, and an uncle who founded the Athenæum library. The most negative influence on young James Storrow was another uncle, A. Lawrence Lowell, who, on a commission named for him, refused to pardon Sacco and Vanzetti, those committed anarchists who were thought to be wrongly convicted of murder. That same Lowell, as a Harvard president, had famously imposed restrictions on the number of Jews and African Americans who could enter Harvard. And that uncle's bigotry had spurred Storrow to become a liberal for life. He had purchased the *Nation* in 1966.

Storrow had an acquisitive mind. He told me about Jessie White Mario, a foreign correspondent for the *Nation* as early as 1866. He related how she had gone from being a nurse in England to covering the revolution in Italy. He said he'd volunteered to tutor disadvantaged elementary-school students

in Harlem. As a copy editor, he could spot errors in fact. Once
he caught a droll misprint in a poet's name: Duane Big Eagle
was spelled "Big Bagel." Another time I found him poring over
the *Oxford English Dictionary* for the word "maven," thinking
it might be spelled like "coven", as in witches. Of course, the
OED did not yield up that Yiddish word.

I wrote for the *Nation*, spurred by their encouragement of
my essays as well as my poetry. My first article for the magazine was "Women the Inventors," based on an idea that had
come to me from memorizing literary figures for interminable
graduate-school exams. I noticed in those lists of authors that
in English and American literature the first writer of every
period and every genre happened to be a woman. Strange but
true, women were the first speakers of Anglo-Saxon poems,
a woman was the first English mystic, the first troubadour,
the first biographer, the first author of a handbook on hunt-
ing, fishing, and hawking. My piece was welcome in 1972, a
breakthrough year for women's rise in professions barred to
them in earlier years. A description of Whitby, home of the
abbess who heard Cædmon sing, brought me in the mail from
an old professor a picture of Pomerania, whose cliffs resembled
Whitby's moors. And Harold Clurman, the drama columnist,
told me stories about the innovative methods of his love, actor
Stella Adler.

In the early 1970s, when hopes for one-world harmony
were at their pinnacle, I wrote about the poetry of other
nations, and acquired translations of poems by Neruda, Yehuda
Amichai, and the Hungarian János Pilinszky. At a time when
Eastern Europe was rife with suffering, I watched a trend
toward poems with a certain bareness of utterance, their lan-

guage evacuated, their lines divested of imagery, allegory, and other devices that could invite subjectivity. Reviewing a book by Michael Hamburger, *The Truth of Poetry*, I was made aware of the struggle of poets like Tadeusz Różewicz, of Poland, to write poetry in the face of silent horror.

There were lighter moments as well. I accepted a poem by the fourteenth-century king Dinis of Portugal, translated by Willard Trask. James read it, and remarked that a poem of any age, if good, was fair game. Still, he teased me about it, calling Dinis "one of the new." And once a poet phoned with a spoof: knowing my flair for the exotic, he disguised his voice as a Pakistani poet.

"Have you read your poems aloud?" I asked, none the wiser.

"Yes," he replied. "We read them—facing East."

It was a long time before I caught on.

While I was at the *Nation*, a friendship with W. S. (William) Merwin began, and it was to be lifelong. He had modestly sent several poems from his forthcoming book, *Writings to an Unfinished Accompaniment*, and, compelled by their beauty, I accepted them all. I didn't know him then, but I suspect it mattered, because he once confided, "I sent five poems to the *New Yorker* and they took them all!" Incredulous, I thought: our foremost American poet, with more books than I had years, is still charged by a magazine acceptance. Suddenly I realized the extent of his passion for poetry, and that it was in me, as well.

He had been my predecessor at the *Nation*, and I'd respected his stand on banning nuclear weapons, his sympathy for the poor, and especially his refusal to sign a loyalty oath that had prevented him from giving a moneyed reading at the State University of New York (SUNY) at Buffalo. When we met, I found him to be reserved, as though protective of his privacy to write, which he did with the miracle of excellence. In time he shed that mask, and shared with me his deepest concerns, such as his devotion to animals. "They take back their own, just wait and see," he said once, referring to a mutual friend who shot grouse in England. On our walks through the Village, there wasn't a dog we passed that William didn't greet. Once, in a shop we entered, he studied a terrier, lifted it to him, and looked into the dog's eyes as though searching for its ancestors.

Soon William was a jolly companion. Although he lived in Hawaii, where he tended acres of palms, he visited New York often, staying in his apartment near Sheridan Square. We drank wine at the home of his editor, Harry Ford. We rode to his Zendo in Riverdale, New York, where in 1983 I was to attend his beautiful Zen Buddhist wedding to Paula Schwartz Merwin. We enjoyed vegetarian dinners. We laughed, or we got angry at whatever government was in power. In all those years, I never heard William speak condescendingly or bitterly, a quality I found refreshing in a major poet.

The new life was uplifting, though old ties remained. In 1972, when he heard of Marianne Moore's death, Jerry rushed to my door. We went with my parents to be with her body on view, in a chapel of the First Presbyterian Church, on Eleventh Street and Fifth Avenue, a short walk from my home. We sat next to Frances Steloff, all five of us secular Jews mourning our Presbyterian elder, Marianne. I recited to myself "What Are Years," one of her poems I'd memorized. In my mind's ear, she was repeating what she'd told me about the poem's punctuation. "It's a meditation," she had said. "I don't want the question mark, and yet they insist on printing it that way." I heard the title with an exclamation mark.

> He
>   sees deep and is glad, who
>   accedes to mortality
>   and in his imprisonment rises
>   upon himself as
>   a sea in a chasm

Her words echoed, and they defied my understanding that her mind could stop. Before the fatal crash of Jerry's parents, death was an abstraction, a man with a scythe. Now here it was again, the real thing.

Late in 1972, the 92nd Street Y phoned, and that phrase alone distinguishes it from the *Nation*: the Y was run by a "we" ensconced in the anonymity of committees; the *Nation* was written and produced by individuals with names, James Storrow, Carey McWilliams, Victor Navasky, Katrina vanden Heuvel. Even the workers who sorted mail were acknowledged on the masthead. The *Nation* had made me strong by insisting on editorial autonomy, refusing to judge, much less to censor, an editor's work; the Y wasn't used to editorial independence. Nevertheless, I agreed to direct its Poetry Center, deciding that, to make time for my jobs there, at Baruch and at the *Nation,* I would simply give up personal life. At PEN, the writers' organization, I joined efforts to free poets jailed in dictatorships. Considering my obligations, Omus Hirshbein, who headed the

Y's performing-arts department, allowed me, as Poetry Center Director, to go to the office only twice a week while keeping in touch with a full-time assistant. It was an exciting time. I built the Y's Discovery competition into Discovery/The Nation, a contest for new poets whose work would be read at the Y and would simultaneously appear in the magazine.

When I was new to the job, Joseph Brodsky broke me in, effectively canceling any hesitations I might have had. Brodsky, whom I'd asked to read at the Y in 1973, took me to a Chinese restaurant beforehand in his newly acquired Cadillac. He'd been taught to drive it by Professor Carl Proffer, his friend and sponsor in Michigan. Brodsky had entered the United States in 1972, free at last from Soviet persecution. That evening, one year after being expelled from his country, he spoke of his apartment in New York, not far from me, in the West Village. Over Chinese noodles, I showed him the poems of Natalya Gorbanevskaya in Daniel Weissbort's translations, which I'd accepted for the *Nation*. Brodsky said that for protesting in Red Square she had been sent to Siberia and subjected to tranquilizers—the same punishment he had been given. For all he had been through, I found him charming and amiable. When he read at the Y, he asked what I thought. "No shit," he was quick to add. I had only praise for his rich, deep voice insinuating Russian tones in his English translations. I heard, too, a rare lack of bitterness, and a kind of qualified faith in the future. No shit.

Some writers read at the Y on "national nights" made up of poetry and music. For the event celebrating the poems of Jalaluddin Rumi, Merwin and Talât Sait Halman read his translations and were followed onstage by a whirling dervish from

Turkey. Before Edmund Keeley's reading of his versions of C. P. Cavafy, a musician played Greek songs on a bouzouki.

When Seamus Heaney, later the Nobel laureate, gave a reading of his poetry at the Y, a guitarist played Irish songs. Afterward, at a reception in my apartment, Seamus's guests sang. I was reminded of Jerry's and my Sundays in Washington Square Park: here each guest would take a turn individually, on impulse, with a preface, such as, "Here's a song my grandfather and I sang together in Sligo, as we did the dishes." To everyone's surprise, Elizabeth Bishop, who came to the reading and the party, joined in with a song she called "Laundry," consisting of shirts, socks, towels, sheets, and other laundry items, and set to the tune of "Yankee Doodle."

In dramatic contrast to Seamus's reception, Yehuda Amichai and his Israeli friends uttered no songs; instead they sat around a table in my apartment arguing somberly about the tense political situation in the Middle East.

James Baldwin's guests argued about books. His performance had been so powerful that I felt the world was listening. He read blues poems, and, at my request, passages from *Go Tell It on the Mountain*. I'd devoured the classic when it came out in 1953, struck by the cry of a character named John, "astonished beneath the power of the Lord." And here was James, a small, thin man with a voice like thunder, delivering language at once biblical and fresh.

Then, as it sometimes happened, the evening's party guests spoke differently. Good-book, bad-book quarrels persisted, while James smiled, aloof from squabbles, gracious and understanding. Suddenly Darryl Pinckney, the novelist, retreated to the bedroom. Although I never found out exactly why, I guessed that, like me, he'd wanted to cherish Baldwin's celestial tones and mute the talk that followed. His privacy was interrupted when Baldwin's secretary entered the room: Darryl fled to my closet, and recalled later, writing in the *New York Review of Books*, that he'd been "hiding among dresses with organdy sleeves."

I reveled in the job as director, even when it demanded hard tasks, such as brewing tea for Allen Ginsberg, who desired a tea ceremony for his followers before the reading, complete with chants and prayer. We provided Earl Grey oolong, despite the Y's traditional coffee brewed in a stainless steel urn that must have served W. H. Auden. Tea had its precedent, for I. B. Singer's wife, Alma, had filled glasses for us before his reading in the European way of her time. But Ginsberg had an Asian Buddhist routine that required its own preparation. When the ritual was over, Ginsberg, who had declined the Scotch offered in yet another Y tradition, furtively downed a glass of it before going on stage. At a party in my apartment, Ginsberg met Isabella Gardner, who mentioned her marriage to Allen Tate. Ginsberg exclaimed, "I didn't know that. Why did you leave him? Did he drink too much?"

"No."

"Did you drink too much?"

"No, drinking had nothing to do with it." That night Ginsberg left, whistling "Here Comes the Bride."

I was a fly on the wall, a voyeur peering into the cracks and fissures of great writers such as Robert Lowell, May Swenson, Maxine Kumin, and Cynthia Ozick. From the wings I watched Galway Kinnell revise, and even compose, poems while reading them on the podium. I heard poems read to

drumbeats by Léopold Sédar Senghor, poet and president of
Senegal, whose performance was preceded by police with dogs
sniffing for bombs. Andrei Voznesensky, the Russian poet, asked
for a real Renoir and a Jean Arp sculpture from the Guggenheim
Museum as stage props for his reading. I couldn't provide them,
but his reason evoked sympathy: he'd wanted such treasures to
impress the Soviet authorities into granting him further leaves.
Oriana Fallaci, the beautiful Italian journalist who covered wars
and once was shot and left for dead, had to be flown in first-
class because "I get crushed in coach." And on the contrary,
Mary McCarthy and Robert Lowell, writers known elsewhere
for their social unpredictability, were courteous, amiable, and
undemanding.

It was always fun to bring the Y programs to Baruch College,
and the writers usually were pleased to be invited. Many of
the students had never before heard a live reading. They liked
to converse in Spanish with Octavio Paz and Mark Strand. The
advanced students were engrossed, and even the uninitiated
applauded: one very young freshman asked Mary McCarthy,
who had just read from *The Stones of Florence*, "Did you write
that yourself?"

"Yes."

"*Very* good."

I expected to hear a rebuke from one of America's prized,
and sometimes ironic, writers. Instead, McCarthy smiled and
thanked her, respect in her tone.

Octavio Paz, who would become a Nobel laureate, came
from Mexico to read his poems in Spanish and in perfect
English. The trip, with his beautiful wife Marie-José, was
planned after my essay on Paz, "Man of Two Worlds," appeared

in the *Hudson Review*. When Frederick Morgan and Paula Deitz first assigned me the task, I confessed that I had scant knowledge of his work. "It will grow," Fred said. Sure enough, I read his books and was enthralled. "If his poetry incarnates the mind's journey toward insight, his voyage is my voyage, his passion my passion," I wrote. Mysteriously, the essay showed up, translated into Spanish, in a Mexican journal.

Through it all I wrote and sent poems to a world that either welcomed them or barred the door. I became accustomed to rejection letters; three in one day hardly fazed me. Then my life changed with yet another surprise phone call. In 1975 Jerry Sherwood, an editor, phoned to announce that Princeton University Press would publish my first book of poems, *Burn Down the Icons*, in their Contemporary Poets series. The choice was made by Theodore Weiss, the series editor, who had been my teacher at Bard College.

My father flew in from a business meeting in Texas to join my mother and me for drinks at the Gramercy Park Hotel, near my office at Baruch. I was to dedicate the book "*To* Jerome Schulman, and *for* my parents, Marcella and Bernard Waldman."

After publication, an unexpected response came from Alfred Corn in the *New York Times Book Review*. I didn't know him at the time, though later we became friends. He liked the book, though that was secondary. What mattered most was that he *got* it. I'd come through at last. When the collection appeared, I was amused by life's peculiarities. My wish to be a news reporter was only the second reason I'd left Bard. The first was that I couldn't reach Ted's standards. My poems were judged not good enough to get me into a workshop.

Now I'm one of Ted's first choices, along with Robert Pinsky and Leonard Nathan. Plus that a stranger named Alfred Corn knows my deepest feelings and sends blessings. I'm grateful for second chances—in poetry, and to come, in marriage.

With permission from Baruch, I taught classes in creative writing at Princeton University for two semesters, and those plus my normal duties made for crowded but exhilarating days. I was fascinated by the broadly interdisciplinary ethos on campus. Robert Fagles, the great translator, was both enlightening and humorous about Homer and Sophocles; Joyce Carol Oates invited me to a lecture by Julian Jaynes, on the bicameral mind. No subject was off-limits to writers and artists. Once my book was sent by mistake to Dr. Manfred Halpern, professor of politics, instead of Daniel Halpern, the editor of *Antaeus*. Rather than send it back, Dr. Halpern read it, contacted me, and arranged a meeting to discuss our use of the same images for different purposes, his for an objective history of civilization, mine for a personal view of reality. I thanked poetry for its long, far-reaching arm.

Because of my book, and others that followed, I felt caught between dedication to my own writing and dedication to that of others. The dilemma, if it was one, would never be resolved. Nor did I heed inner warnings to stand still.

10

PARALLEL LIVES

*I*n a photo of Jerry and me on a beach in bright sun, we stand
separate, he searching the land, I looking out at the ocean, our
shadows trailing behind us on the sand, merged into one being. I
think of Plato, who tells us that we human beings were created
with four arms and legs, and a head with two faces. Fearing our
power, Zeus split us into separate parts, condemning us to spend
lives looking for the other half.

I can think of no better way to describe Jerry's presence
during the seventies, when I opted for an independent life. Why,
in the midst of a powerful anti-war speech by Senator George
McGovern, I imagine Jerry's reserved though enthusiastic
response. Why, walking diagonally across Washington Square
Park in daylight, on my way to the Nation's offices, then on
Sixth Avenue at Fourth Street, I'm transported to one of our
walks on that same path at night under a full moon, singing
"Wildflowers," from The Golden Apple, a musical we'd gone
back to see a second time. Why, completing a new poem, I absent-

mindedly leave it on "Jerry's table," which he used for mail. Why,
seeing El Greco's painting of Jerry's namesake and look-alike,
Saint Jerome, at the Metropolitan Museum, I frighten another
viewer by crying out, "Speak!"

And when was it born, this two-headed creature now split
apart? Or was it always there, as Plato thought? I date its incep-
tion from when, on a trip to Martinique, Jerry surfaced from the
bay where he'd been snorkeling to look after a child at our little
auberge who was howling from pain in her leg, probably frac-
tured. Her father, the manager, had called an ambulance that was
slow in arriving. Then he shouted for Jerry. Still wet from the bay
and in his swimming trunks, wearing a beach towel like a prayer
shawl, Jerry stayed with the girl until help came, holding her face
in his hands, speaking softly to her.

It's not that I miss his presence, just that I see him unexpectedly in real and remembered scenes. In 1968 in Iowa, the
best man at Dick Yates's wedding to Martha Speer, he stands
beside Dick at the university chapel, the two men erect, sol-
emn, hopeful. After the ceremony, Jerry leans down to escort
the little flower girl up the aisle. And today I board a cross-
town bus and see him, outside the window, bending down to
stroke a Labrador retriever.

Though we kept separate quarters, Jerry and I met frequently,
shared disasters, attended ceremonies. Our love was intact,
our meetings harmonious. Once, in a heavy storm, unwilling
to cancel Michael Harper's performance at the Y ("We don't
cancel in this business," Omus Hirshbein had ruled), I trudged
home for six miles in the snow from the Y on Ninety-Second
Street to University Place. Jerry had been roasting potatoes

in the oven and gave me one, uncut and in its skin, wrapped in a paper towel, at the door. "For the warm," he said. On another evening, Jerry attended a party at the apartment after a reading given by Czeslaw Milosz. When invited, Jerry had said, "I'll get there early and take the Fontina out of the fridge." Talking to Milosz, he sensed that the poet wanted more to eat than the cheese and the pâté that I offered. Jerry spontaneously sautéed veal chops for a delighted Czeslaw, and then joined the conversation. Milosz, who had been raised a Catholic in Poland, later an exile, was talking of his interest in Jewish culture, and of his wish to read Hebrew poetry in its new English translations.

Sometimes, during our so-called separation, our activities were parallel, if not entirely enmeshed. Jerry had applauded my work for PEN protesting the imprisonment of writers in dictatorships. And one afternoon in 1977, Jerry told me he would be joining a protest march, sponsored by the Committee of Concerned Scientists, to allow Dr. Benjamin Levich, a Russian physicist, an exit visa he'd been denied for a trip to Israel. "It's what you do," Jerry said. "You and I both," he added. Together we celebrated Levich's release in 1978, but lamented that the Soviets made him relinquish citizenship.

Shortly after Levich was freed, my father succumbed to an arteriosclerosis attack that was to end his life in 1980. During his last years, Jerry supervised his medical care, assisted my mother, and scheduled home-care aides. At his funeral service in the Riverside Memorial Chapel, Jerry sat in the family row, holding my hand throughout. Afterward, he criticized the rabbi for a self-centered service, but thanked Ashley Montagu, my father's longtime friend, for a touching eulogy. Ashley greeted Jerry warmly, knowing of his attachment to my father. He reminded us of how he'd accompanied my parents to our apartment after Jerry's poor mother was killed in the head-on traffic collision. He recalled that when Jerry had thanked them for coming, my father replied, "Of course. You're my son."

Why Jerry and I did not reunite was a question we silently asked ourselves. The short answer was that we weren't ready to combine our lives. The longer one was that we guessed there would be time. Jerry was often away on science journeys, which I suspect was only partially true. I did not know the whole of it, but could hazard a guess: he was a handsome man, and women were not immune to his charm. Earlier in our marriage, I'd laugh at an attractive young woman's intent stare, or at the occasional flirting at parties, the tentative advances. One woman, the wife of a playwright I knew, had phoned him at our apartment while we'd been hosting a party. She said she was visiting Greenwich Village and asked him to meet her downstairs. He didn't leave that night, but I suspected he'd been seeing her during our times apart. And now, after the break, I was confident in the strength of our bond. One evening late I phoned him at his Perry Street apartment with the news that Willard Trask, a beloved mutual friend by then, had died. No answer, no message machine. I shrugged: I'd chosen my life. I never phoned again.

Nor did I languish alone during those years. There were encounters that sometimes grew into friendships. Talking with Derek Walcott, the great Caribbean poet, I understood the tension of double loyalties. He wrote powerfully of the twin allegiances to Africa of his heritage and to the English language and culture he loved, despite Britain's harsh colonial policy.

I heard in his lines concerns for the Jews, also divided, faithful to languages of their adopted countries. Once he read poems that overwhelmed me for their urgency and their likeness to the plight of my ancestors. Listening backstage, I grabbed what I thought was a long-stemmed rose and steered it to him. He reached for it, felt its texture, and declared, "You've given me a fake rose!" It was a prop from a play. It was symbolic of my failure to tell Derek how much his poems meant to me. I could do so only years later, in a poem I wrote called "Division," in which I identify my own double loves with his "language of British rule and music of patois." My poem ends:

> I send this to you as a poet
> wrote to Li Po from a street in Warsaw,
> in the learned Yiddish of my ancestors,
> asking for a poem of praise. And fear.

I wanted to give him the book it was in, *Without a Claim*, saying "This rose is real." But by then, in 2014, he'd been ill and was too weak to reply.

T. Carmi, an Israeli poet, was another visitor. He read his poems in Hebrew and in a proper English enlivened by street slang. No wonder: he had been born and raised in the Bronx, and at age twenty had immigrated to Jerusalem. Hebrew became his writing language, and subsequently he could not translate his own poems. I went to work on them.

Although I had only rudimentary Hebrew, I took a course, read, went to Israel during the summers, and conversed with guests where I stayed at the Mishkenot Sha'ananim, a residence for artists in Yemin Moshe, Jerusalem. It was intensive work. Carmi gave me alternates for nearly every word I had to render into English, inking them on worksheets with phonetic pronunciations. Then, at our meetings, he read them aloud. "Let the voice inside tell you what to choose," he said. And I chose largely by ear. The result was his book I translated into English, *At the Stone of Losses.*

Carmi had just finished editing *The Penguin Book of Hebrew Verse,* a hefty anthology in which he traces an unbroken line of poetry from pre-biblical times to the present. He spoke of cultures that knew the art, including the Italian Renaissance, the Andalusian poetic empire, Muslim Spain. I was enthralled.

Unlike Jerry, Carmi would not have won prizes for physical beauty. Until he spoke, he was hardly noticed in a crowd. He chain-smoked, a habit which led to an early death. He was untidy with cigarette ashes; his hair was uncombed; and his hands always looked dirty, whether or not they were. And yet the language of his poems was lavishly romantic, seductive in subtle ways.

Besides, translation is erotic. It can arouse a love that is passionate, familial, selfless, or a combination of the three. Whether eros is acted upon or sublimated doesn't matter. It's there. Shakespeare said it best in Sonnet 111: "my nature is subdu'd / to what it works in, like the dyer's hand." Defer to the work. The dye has the same root—*inficire*—as infection, another word used in Sonnet 111. A good translator can adhere to the work, and then to its creator. My mother had subdued her nature to the men she aided—her father, and later, her husband. Her marriage was successful, though I still feel her regrets about lost independence. My deference was to what I worked in, the minds of people far away.

Whitman wrote: "My dearest dream is for an internationality of poems and poets binding the lands of the earth closer than all treaties or diplomacy." Let someone else have that noble calling, Mark Strand or Alastair Reid. As for me, after dipping my hand in dye for Carmi and, later, for the Nicaraguan poet Pablo Antonio Cuadra, I gave up laboring in the art that I still believe in.

After our work was finished, the book published, and a *Present Tense* prize for translation from Hebrew awarded to me, I met Mahmoud Darwish, a Palestinian poet, at an international conference sponsored by PEN. In our first conversation, I learned of a curious ambivalence. To be sure, Darwish and Carmi stood on either side of the famous Middle Eastern divide. But they were more like loving cousins than enemies. They looked alike. They shared the same expressions, the same humor, the same *culture*.

Darwish knew that Carmi, who had fought for Israel's independence in 1948, later became an advocate for peace. The Palestinian Darwish knew Carmi's poems in the original Hebrew, as he did Yehuda Amichai's, and he made me aware of the tenderness existing among many writers from Israel, Palestine, and the Arab countries. "We translate each other into our own languages," he said, over cranberry juice at the St. Moritz bar. In that same meeting, he asked me to read aloud translations of his poems in an event featuring his colleagues from Poland, Russia, Yugoslavia, and Spain. I said, "I'm honored, but how could I fill your expectations, since I am a woman and a Jew?" He replied by translating an Arabic expression that moves me to this day: "You are my family. Be one of my family."

Again friends were urging me to relinquish obligations and get

117

back to writing my own poems, which the Y duties had slowed to a standstill. After he read my third book, *For That Day Only*, William Merwin chided me for allowing the hiatus. He admonished me to arrange a schedule that would accommodate my poetry. Merwin was to refer to my too-busy life in his late poem "Testimony," in which he leaves me:

> the sounds of an invisible
> river rushing around her there
> that she hears now that she is standing still.

By then I had followed his advice. Although I liked being an enabler, I knew that I was only one of thousands who enjoyed those events. I was expendable. Did Italo Calvino remember how I coached his English, rescuing him from pronouncing "stalactite" as "stalack-titty"? Recently I visited a photographic retrospective at the Y to find that I was cropped out of a Thomas Victor photograph taken before a performance in the Green Room, where I had been talking with Jorge Luis Borges and W. S. Merwin. No matter. I cherished the memory: Borges had asked if I was Jewish, because he intended to read a story he'd just written about Jews in Argentina. Then William had inquired whether Borges knew that Milton had written "Methought I saw my late espoused saint" without ever having seen his wife. Borges, blind, looked up from his chair and replied, "Yes, but he did in his mind."

No, I don't regret the cropping of that photo. Instead, I think of those nights, smile, and silently exclaim, wasn't that a glorious time!

11

BLIND MOLES

One night in 1975, after some weeks away, Jerry was at the Y, unannounced. I spotted him in the audience, at a poetry-and-science event I'd organized that included Lewis Thomas and Muriel Rukeyser. Jerry had introduced me to Thomas's essays when they first appeared in the *Journal of American Medicine*. When they were reprinted in his book *The Lives of a Cell: Notes of a Biology Watcher*, I was startled to find that the scientist used some of the same imagery for cell fusion as Rukeyser used in her book *The Life of Poetry*. Both wrote passionately, and in like manner, about the unity of all living things. I wrote an article about it called "Songs of Our Cells" for the *Hudson Review*. And now they were reading at the Y.

"Unprecedented," Jerry exclaimed to me afterward. "My medical students were there taking notes." He was drawn to my work at the Y, and had attended other talks unrecognized, he said, such as a reading by Octavio Paz and a lecture by the microbiologist René Dubos.

"You know you started me on it. Many ideas, in fact."

"What about dinner?"

"It's a school night. I should get back."

We met several times a week after that, traveled to the Caribbean winters, and once, to Tuscany, where we gazed at several paintings of the Annunciation, the Virgin at her writing desk apprised of Christ's coming. And before each one we the childless were struck by the miracle of birth.

Our marriage continued in that way for years, though we still lived separately. It always seemed there would be time to formally integrate our lives. My frequent escort was Arthur Gregor. Once an editor at Macmillan, he brought me to Bach recitals of his friend, the pianist Rosalyn Tureck, and to the lively house of Ruth Nanda Anshen, a philosopher who edited science books and entertained their authors. He also introduced me to Nina and Herman Schneider, who instantly became my friends. At their home I met Robert Phelps, a tall, languid man whose quiet, conversational tones contrasted with his fervent passion for Colette, whose works he translated. He loved to gossip and to devour Nina's veal roast, but frequently interrupted both pleasures to ask about my poems, asserting the importance of creative lifework. And at one of Nina's small parties, her guest Philip Roth entertained the group with a high humor that seemed effortless, reminding me of a lithe dancer who performed unexpected, elegant turns.

When Arthur moved to France, I visited him and his partner, Richard, and we traveled to the abbey at Saint-Benoît-sur-Loire, where the poet Max Jacob had hidden before he was arrested as a Jew and taken to Drancy.

One day—it is hard to say when—the realization came that the tensions Jerry and I once had were gone, and our times together were shimmering with laughter. The woman I'd become had left in the rubble the child of the fifties. That night, after a dinner of corned beef sandwiches at the Second Avenue Deli, then on Tenth Street in the East Village, he sat in silence. He stammered as he always did in times of intense emotion.

"Might we—I mean, as we are now—that is, if we—you know—why not—oh, damn!"

As Jerry spoke, his eyes widened. It was as though he aimed at oration and delivered broken phrases instead. His voice cracked, out of tune.

I didn't help him out. His faltering speech was giving me time to think. He wants to come home. He loves me. And yet he was always there, regardless of arrangement. He had my first book's dedication, as he would the second, and probably others. I'd read of a sign in Jung's studio: *Vocatus atque non vocatus Deus aderit* ("Summoned or not summoned, God will be there").

"I mean—unless you wanted—wouldn't it be easier on our friends, your parents, my brother's family?"

"You want to get back together," I finally said, breaking the silence.

"Yes." He sat back, relieved, spreading more Russian dressing on his rye bread.

"What about your other, er, attachments?"

He smiled and said nothing. I offered my credit card to cover half the check. He declined the card, remembering, perhaps, that I hadn't one when we'd parted. "Let's meet this weekend. There's a revival of a movie you liked at the Art. *Paths of Glory*."

I'm home alone. He wants to reunite. He's asked before, but now he stammers deep feeling. Or does the stammer mean hesitation? Is that a warning? Or is it fascination? We're married. We're in love. Why ask for more? And what about my hard-won independence? Would this move chain us together like convicts, plunging me back into the slough that depressed us both? But now we're older, my independence is real. Women have equality. Freedom. My mother is vindicated. And yet.

That Saturday, dressing for the movie in jeans and a V-neck Shetland he'd given me, I saw flashing before me the white-to-purple hydrangeas on our first walk through the park. I thought of our ambles through Paris, our races through Turkey and Greece. Jerry walked in the door. His long legs were in chinos and a red-blue striped shirt shone bright against his fair skin. His face lighted up when he smiled, the corners of his eyes crinkling, in just the way I had remembered. He settled fire-red roses on a table, and kissed me. The stammer was gone, and his voice rang like deep bells. "Ready to go?" he asked.

"Yes," I said. "And yes, I'll help you move."

The apartment did not change, as a visitor pointed out when she heard he was back to stay. Jerry kept few possessions other than his smart Brooks jackets, his box of No. 2 pencils, his science journals, and his music CDs, which were mostly in his car. Nor did I, apart from a long wall of floor-to-ceiling books. Unlike my mother, who doted on her porcelain shepherd, and her Kunisada print with its red stamp showing it was real, I preferred to keep objects scarce. Jerry was touched, however, when he noticed I had kept a wooden bowl he'd found while doing medical fieldwork in the Dominican Republic, long before our marriage. While I disregarded his instructions to never wash it even when soiled ("Simply rub it with a garlic clove"), I did keep the bowl, unused, cracked, and discolored.

Jerry had come back into my life, and my life was eager to have him. My friends, too, applauded our recovery. The poet Richard Howard, who lived one block away on Mercer Street, took me aside at the local copy center to say, "You've gotten back together with a man your friends can stand, and that's got to be salubrious."

What friends did not know was that our renewed marriage, though loving, even blissful at times, was never easy. But, then, I've come to regard happiness as embracing what you have—and then what you have left. Both are incomplete, part sun, part haze, part darkness. The return only seemed easier for Jerry, by the looks of his jovial demeanor. Actually, it was harder. In the years we lived apart I'd had brief involvements, and was happy to "forsake all others" for the marriage. He had one attachment, and it was of longer duration. He had been less open about his evenings away than I was about my friendships, and he continued visiting her even after we reunited.

Here, in the interests of accuracy, I must acknowledge that I've changed the name and precise circumstances of the following account. She was a doctor he'd met on rounds in an AIDS unit. I'd met her only once, at a party, and saw her run the back of her hand along his shoulder.

Their meetings were hidden, like the paths made by blind moles under a well-kept lawn. Months—or was it years?—

after he moved back in 1983, I became aware: an overheard phone conversation, a blow to the head, my heart hit hard. Questions shot through me as though I'd seen a building fall and slip into the earth. The hole. Scattered metal parts, broken glass. You know what's happened, but do not understand it.

He denied the affair, trying a feeble cover-up, "Clarisse at the lab. She always talks affectionately, means nothing by it." A week later, after shuddering nervously in classes, I found a tattered index card with the name Linda and an unfamiliar address on his dressing table, left there casually, as though waiting for me to notice it. Strange, but the story gets even stranger as I follow the clues.

To love someone means you don't bolt when you find his car parked outside an Upper West Side building, thinking he's at a conference in another city. To be loved by him is when he comes back contrite and begs to make amends. I went into a restaurant across the street and spotted them, two people behaving in the eagerly probing yet familiar way of an established pair. He invited me to join them, introduced me to Linda, then lurched toward the door and went home, saying it would be too painful to stay. I stayed, wanting to know more. She looked older than I'd anticipated, or perhaps her facial creases were deepened by anxiety. Truth came in punches: "I didn't know he was married" and "We were planning a long trip." As it came out, she had accepted him in 1970 as a married lover, urged our separation, and assumed we were living apart. On her side, she had been misled with false promises and expectations.

Then the anger. At times during this awful year, I laugh at the change, hero scientist to common prowler. Discovery in science becomes discovery of betrayal. Weekends away for panel discussions of dendritic cells, site-visit schedules. The plane delays, the car needing repair. My denial. The phone calls from distant places. I see him now: By day the good doctor, by night a witch doctor behind a mask with eye-slits, to see and not be seen. Superman in a phone booth, changing to Clark Kent. The curtain raised on a monster with three heads and six serpent eyes it would take another Heracles to slay. Our marriage with the roots of a flowering zinnia that blooms in lie. The statue in bronze turned green with rust.

Jerry and I had it out. In one of our fraught conversations, confined to late afternoons in what we ironically called "happy hours," he said that Linda had worshipped him uncritically.

"Was I too critical?"

"Yes, your feelings are hurt when I tell you the soup isn't hot enough."

"Come now, was I too critical?

"Yes . . . no. My mother, was. Oaf. That's what she called me. Oaf." A picture came to my mind of a major Thanksgiving dinner Jerry had prepared before our marriage in his walkup apartment. In a "Pullman" kitchen with a screen hiding stove, sink, and fridge, he roasted a turkey, soaked cranberries for sauce, and filled a Pyrex dish with marshmallow-covered yams. Shirley, his mother, had only one response: "He should have been a girl."

"She tore me down." When he made high school valedictorian, topping even his brother with a starry grade average, his mother had gone to the school to find out if they'd made a mistake.

Then the crash, her death in the car his father drove.

And Shirley had been misused from girlhood. Like my mother, she hungered for an education after she'd done well in a rigorous city high school. Unlike my mother, she worked for low wages and married a man who did not return her affection. Harshness came full circle. Those who break the circle have strength of character. He was to break the circle by not using his past to excuse his wrongs.

"I engineered that discovery," he said. "I wanted it." Together we found a family therapist who helped us talk freely to one another. After a few sessions, he went into a deep analysis. What impressed me was his refusal to let the wrongs done to him excuse his actions. His guilt was a life sentence, just as my years-long denial was mine. I had looked away, fearful of disturbing my marriage. I decried his bad behavior, and so did he. The bare realization was that human nature is flawed. Truth, though essential, is not always uplifting. But finally, I admired his character. He fought for redemption with courage and dignity. He never saw her again. He heard she'd moved to Houston, Texas, to marry a composer and work in the Baylor College of Medicine there. His relief matched mine.

The betrayal had its fallout. Try as I might, I couldn't get my mind around forgiveness.

"What about trust?" he implored.

"Hell, no."

"What do you feel?"

"I'm your wife and I love you."

"I'll take that."

12

THE HEART

Gradually we became able to gaze at the good, as at a painting whose artist smudged out lines and didn't cover them entirely with new paint. In my experience, the phrase "happy marriage" is a term of opposites, like "friendly fire" or "famous poet." My marriage has been a feast of contradiction: radiance and dissatisfaction; intense loyalties and devastating treacheries; freedom and the sacrifice, albeit willing, of independence; excitement and a kind of pleasant boredom. And fury, irrational by definition, the syllables pouring out unchecked. While we had no answers, we both believed, in calm moments, there had to be a way of talking peace. That, together with profound love, pulled us through.

Our marriage renewed, a constant regret was that we hadn't gotten back sooner. Close as we'd been, we missed out. On his science trip to Moscow. To Milan. On my option to take him to the White House in 1980 when I was received by President and Mrs. Carter in "A Salute to Poetry and

American Poets." Hearing of my White House adventure, Jerry had been jubilant for me. "Just to think that you, a kid born in Brooklyn, with an eye infection, gets to go to the White House." That day I had lacked Jerry the most poignantly when I talked with other couples, James and Annie Wright, May Swenson and Zan Knudson. How he would have been amused by Zan's comment, as she approached the hors d'oeuvres: "I want to see what grub they have here." How, with his spider's eye, he might have observed details I didn't take in.

After the crisis and its therapy, we were able to talk of what for years we had referred to as "our infertility," unbound by the stiffness of the early sixties. Jerry's testicular defect that resulted in sterility—no sperm, not even one—shadowed his life: no miracle of birth, no genes, no geniuses, no heirs, no immortality—in our religion, children to speak our names after death. At the outset, both of us were divided about adoption, but differently: He wanted it and yet feared it would be a reminder of the cause. I, though fearful of being unfulfilled, was also relieved. Now there would be no diapers, no sticky plums, no dumped ice-cream cones, and the bonus of extended writing time.

Benighted in 1962, we could not talk about how the sperm test had awakened his sexual fears. He'd felt inadequate. Gradually he abstained. All he'd said was "Just call us Jake Barnes and Brett Ashley," referring to Hemingway's couple, in *The Sun Also Rises*, who love one another despite a war wound that prevents sex.

It was unfortunate for our early marriage that we were unable to say openly how we felt. Now we could, too late for our nonexistent children but not too late for us, and for the entirety of our good days and nights.

Danger lay ahead. In September 1985, when Jerry was fifty-eight, he was in New Jersey on a laboratory consultation when he felt severe chest pain. He embarked on the three-hour drive back to New York City and the Mount Sinai Hospital emergency room. On the way he suffered a heart attack, a myocardial infarction, and continued driving to Mount Sinai, where he was admitted. "Please bring my blue pajamas" was his phoned request, and I did. His internist told me he'd neglected his health, canceling appointments which might have put off the event. Late though it was, however, his life was saved. When he recovered from the attack, he was advised to have balloon angioplasty, new at the time, at St. Luke's in Kansas City, one of the few hospitals to take on the procedure. I called off classes to accompany him. After I'd spent some time in the waiting room, an expansive area near a green atrium, his doctor came to me and said, "We can't do it. We've tried and we're tired. He must go back to New York and have bypass surgery." Bypass then was also a relatively new method. "What will happen if he doesn't?" I asked, fumbling for words that would hide my disappointment. "Sudden death," he answered, in a clipped tone.

Compose yourself. Calm down before you see him. If those words, "sudden death," ring in my *head, they must be sirens in his.* I left the waiting room for the Episcopal chapel, on the ground floor. Of course I still held tightly to Judaism, but the Healing Service at St. Luke's Chapel, then in progress, was a gift.

When bidden, I walked to the altar. The priest put his hand on my head and offered prayers "for Jerome," a man he didn't know, then for me. To this day, I can't help but suspect it turned my husband's care. Luke, patron saint of artists and physicians, had to be looking out for us. I went back upstairs, refreshed, to Jerry's hospital room, where I found him sitting straight up and watching a football game on TV. "He'll be all right," the surgeon confided, no longer confessing that his heart team was tired. "He had us do it again. It worked." Jerry explained what had happened. Lying on his gurney in the operating room, he'd argued that statistically the percentage of successful angioplasties exactly matched the unsuccessful, and that they should give it another shot. And so they did. "The patient is always right," the surgeon admitted wryly. I knew, however, that the real Healer was one Jerry could never believe in. Nor I, most of the time. This was exceptional. A miracle.

His heart restored, Jerry survived on pills in white bottles, blue bottles, and see-through canisters. Every night, every morning, he spread a panoply of bottles on the bed. They contained green capsules, yellow tablets, and orange caplets. He counted them out as though numbering the days.

Despite the heart condition, his life and work went on as usual. The good times grew better. When we lay in bed lovingly, the early past was muted. I concentrated on the moment: Tonight Mozart, with the music flowing through our bodies. Tomorrow night, Mahler. The full moon illuminating a country road; a lamppost lighting a city street.

Nor did the brush with mortality shorten our sense of time. There was time to enjoy the Conservatory Garden in

Central Park, across Fifth Avenue from Mount Sinai and Jerry's lab. Like our house, it, too, had a mixed beauty, this one physical: nasturtiums shone, their odor of cocoa mulch tinged with urine, and candy wrappers in the daffodil bed. When Jerry worked at Mount Sinai, I often brought sandwiches at lunchtime and we'd sit on a bench in a crabapple allée talking, perhaps, of the spirea that would bloom in the fall. Once, we watched a young man nearby as he scattered fallen white blossoms on his love's black shoulders, her arms, her wrists. And on another noonday, a child held a daffodil with both hands in wonder—as though this might be her first living, growing flower.

There was time to spend weekends and summers at our house in the rural outback of Springs, on eastern Long Island, near the inlets and bays of the Sound. I'd bought it in 1977, for $40,000 as a minimal cabin, leaks and all, and we later remodeled it in 2000 into a dream house, small but quintessentially ours. The rebuilding had its worries, such as a contractor who razed the cabin, kept asking for more money, and finally pocketed the extra funds and walked off the job. After we reported his foul deed to the town's building committee, John Specht, a carpenter who lived nearby, heard of our plight. He obtained a contractor's license and finished the house with high ceilings, bay windows, a back deck, and an extra room for my studio.

Our lives in city and country called forth a doubling of spirit, with asphalt in one, seashells in the other. Jerry's first addition to the new house was a sound system he'd constructed, with standing speakers and speakers hidden in the high ceilings, an amplifier, a bass box, and numerous colored wires. On winter nights we listened to the Verdi Requiem and to Mendelssohn's *Elijah*. Summers we put music on to celebrate holidays. America's independence was observed with a CD of Charles Ives's *Variations on "America."* *Quatorze Juillet*, Bastille Day, called for Berlioz's "La Marseillaise." One year on July 14, I resurrected a 1959 recording of Édith Piaf singing "Non, je ne regrette rien." About our marriage, that was true. I had no regrets.

We lived on a quiet road, seldom going to the village except for provisions. Oaks and junipers stood in our yard, as well as an American beech tree that never lost its leaves, not even in winter. The land was hospitable to unplanted foliage that grew wild, such as heart-shaped, pink flowers that came as a gift in the droppings of a migrating bird.

The house became a hideaway and a mixed blessing. Perennials in bloom reminded us constantly of passing time, hours we could not bear to lose. The forsythia bloomed yellow in May, announcing spring; the azalea showed its fuchsia in late May. The rhododendron, our "June bride," flourished purple in June, reminding us of how Jerry had planted it as a shrub and we watched it grow higher than our one-story roof. When its time was over, green hooks clawed the air where its blossoms had been. The hydrangeas bloomed an odd mauve-green in August, and by that month the high sunlight of summer-solstice days had lessened, one minute per day. Fire-colored leaves began to cover the grass and had to be raked away. All of our plantings were perennials, and their return every spring, the greens unfurling through ice, inspired in us hope for recurrent seasons of life. At the same time, the question lurking in my mind, still unspoken, was how many more springs we would be on earth to watch the first lilies of the valley unfurl like tiny umbrellas.

His heart symptoms gone, Jerry managed our outdoor grill with the ardor that must have belonged to the first man to use fire. His predilection for birdwatching in nearby Gerard Park, another promontory on Long Island Sound, suited his eye for minute detail. He waited for the ospreys to occupy their nest in March and noted their departures in August. Handing me the binoculars, he'd say "Look for the flicker's spotted head," or "Look for stripes, one for the willet, two for the killdeer." He taught me to notice ruddy turnstones, terns, dowitchers.

As a writer, I had thought of myself as observant, but there was much that I'd missed. Besides, Jerry's birding was entirely of another sort. He ached for it. He gazed upward as though looking for angels, though actually as the scientist studying what he can see. He limped as the egret stalks, but without wings. Though a professed unbeliever, he looked toward heaven. I thought of Saint Thomas's words, "Watch what you know and what is hidden will come clear."

Near Springs, we scrambled on the Walking Dunes, a stretch of sand hills inland, as close to a desert as I can imagine on the North Atlantic coast. From those heights we could see no greenery, no water, only sand. We climbed with our long-time friends Dore Ashton and Matti Megged, and told linked stories, one person picking up another's narrative. Once, when the endless-desert feeling began to cause some wavering in our recitations, we saw lightning flicker through palls of clouds. No sound of thunder yet, just the luminous assurance that water was nearby, the promise that rain would come.

It was in that landscape years later that Jerry and I would mourn the victims of September 11, 2001. We had watched the

towers of the World Trade Center fall as we stood on the roof of
our One University Place, one mile north of the tragedy. Classes
had been canceled in the city's colleges, and the air hung
heavy with smoke and debris. I dreaded the reentry to classes,
remembering one good student who had told me she was an
intern, her father a clerk, in one of the tower's offices.

The next day, we left for Long Island. In our quiet town,
we were reminded of the disaster: tall cedars were towers built
to sway in wind; sand scuffed with footprints was rubble; sun-
clouds darkened, telling us of the smoke-clouds in downtown
New York. Returning to the city after a few days, we found
that terror was signaled by an "orange alert," not yet severe as
red but high, possibly suggesting a new attack.

Later that week, we'd gone to Lincoln Center for a concert
of Dvořák's Symphony No. 9, "From the New World." Settling
into plush, we read in our programs that Dvořák had composed it during a visit to America. "He must have listened to us
hard," Jerry whispered when it began. In the music we heard
strains of Hasidic melodies, African chants, calls and responses,
and "come-thou's," reminding us of how our youthful folk
songs of many nations had expressed our hopes for world harmony. At the end, the audience stood and cheered. The music
won. We still believed.

"I like to think of William and Paula Merwin listening to
Haydn in their garden," Jerry said, referring to a CD we'd
watched them pack to play in Hawaii. William loved New York,
but he preferred to stay "surrounded by palms and birdsong."
When their visits became scarce, we wrote letters. The "garden," he told us, was nineteen acres long, and they'd given it to

a conservancy, hoping to save it into the future.

The garden. Its beauty remains, even in the face of mortality. And even more so in the fall from the illusion of ideal perfection. The garden in our house was a fraction of the Merwins' size, but bright with roses and hydrangeas. For me it represented the Eden of our marriage that only had seemed to be lost at the discovery of reality—like water snakes under a brown carpet of leaves in the woods behind our house. Revelation can jar. Like fire, it can destroy. Or it can heal.

Or in other words, temptation. Early on, William, like Jerry, had wildly good looks. I had envied Paula's placid acceptance when women crowded her William. She reminded me of how, in the early years of our own marriage, I had laughed at the women's attempts. Now, conscious of Jerry's vulnerable nature, I was alert. I also knew he took warmly to flirtation. Once at a New Year's Eve party, Jerry listened so intently to a woman's animated talk that he had to be reminded it was time for our midnight kiss. I was sure of his years-long fidelity, and still I respected Paula's demeanor.

Like William, Jerry had an easygoing manner, both laconic and tough. That may account for why I didn't notice, at first, that Jerry had lost his springy stride. Nor did I observe him when he'd stop to stretch his leg on a tree stump. Instead I saw him as always, long-limbed and rangy, and speaking with a twinkling smile.

It was in the garden, planting impatiens, that he fell and couldn't get to his feet without a neighbor's help. "Stiff," he said, and went back to the house to toss a bean salad for lunch. But he left most of the impatiens in its pots, and never planted again.

It would be months before he'd grimace in pain, squirm in his seat, and murmur in sleep. Meanwhile, he'd drive to our country house and, in the city, attend work and visit friends as usual.

We had gone to the Conservatory Garden right after our friend Irving Howe died, across the street at Mount Sinai. Jerry, who worked at the hospital, was one of the last doctors to see him. I had met Irving for the first time thirteen years before, in 1980, when I interviewed him at the Y about his criticism. We became friends, Irving and his wife, Ilana, Jerry and I. I'd been translating the Carmi poems, and Ilana, an Israeli who knew the originals, read my translations. Together we four went to dinners and concerts, argued about films, agreed about novels. I was charmed by Irving's subtle humor, warmed by his awe of Jerry's dedication to science. When he first went to Mount Sinai, for heart surgery, Jerry became an advocate. "He's an important man," a callow resident had told Jerry. "He's a sick man. Take care of him," Jerry replied, to the resident's shame.

Though Jerry's last visit to Irving's room was social, he was wearing a lab coat that amused Ilana. She called it "Jerry's white robe," her sexy accent drawing out the long "o" in "robe." Shortly before Irving became ill, the four of us had gone to the Garden together, and after Irving died I thought that his soul might be lodged behind a screen of roses, pink to golden in the sun. Later I found out that he had told Ilana in Paris, sitting on a bench between rose shrubs and pointing to them, "I know that death, if it meant coming into those, might be all right."

In that place, I thought of a prayer Irving had recited to me: "Lord, give me life till my work is done, and work till my life is done." "But work is never finished," I'd replied at the time. Now I hoped he'd felt assured that his work was done.

As I thought of Irving's death, I watched Jerry sorting twigs to mend a fallen aster. It was all he could do, frustrated at his inability to keep Irving alive.

We learned of strength in adversity from Hedda Sterne, a Romanian-born abstract expressionist who painted geometric forms bathed in light as though seen from a prism. Throughout her nineties, Hedda would invite us to dinner she prepared in her garden apartment.

Hedda had exquisite insight into character. "Jerry knows where he ends and the other person begins," she observed, referring to his wisdom in approaching others. I had a special fondness for people who had insight into Jerry's character. It was always exhilarating to visit Hedda, whom I'd known since 1977. I'd been invited to collaborate with a local painter in a show called "Poets and Painters" at Guild Hall in East Hampton. I was asked to choose from a list of painters not yet "taken," including Ossorio, de Kooning, and a host of others. I asked a friend, Dore Ashton, to review the list and she said, "Hedda Sterne is not on this sheet." I phoned, and a friendship began. For the show, she painted moon-blanched horizons, and in each horizon she inserted the words of my poem, "Moon." Although the painter was required to use no more than six words of a poem, Hedda displayed the whole poem in the horizon lines.

Hedda spoke in aphorisms so wise that they remain with

me, and I hope will, as long as I live and work. Often she emphasized the gap between the artist and the work: "When you are at your deepest you participate in something beyond and outside of you" or "Art is a recycling of life; my painting, like a lobster who eats trash, has rosy flesh." By 1990, Hedda's failing sight did not interfere with her incessant reading ("Reading in bed at night is like group sex"), or with painting large abstract canvases, or even with preparing dinner for us. "Accuracy is essential in art," she said. "If you're true to the imagination, you may not always be factual but you will be accurate."

We needed her example of fortitude. We also relied on Ted Weiss, my college teacher who'd chosen my book for the Princeton series. He and his wife, Renée, often had us to lunch in Princeton. When talking about poetry, Ted lit up and words poured out, ranging from sage to comical. He had retired from teaching and from editing the *Quarterly Review of Literature* after half a century. His health was poor and he looked frail, but his thoughts still came nonstop, as did his puns. When the Weisses took us to the Institute for Advanced Study, we joined the physicist Freeman Dyson for the noon meal. He and Jerry had an engaging conversation about quantum mechanics. "We came for some good talk and we won't leave until we've had it," Ted remarked.

Once we visited Karl Kirchwey and Tamzen Flanders in Bryn Mawr. Karl, a poet who was my successor at the Y, had joined the Bryn Mawr College faculty in 1990. After that, we drove to the Barnes Foundation while it was still in Merion, Pennsylvania. I had been hesitant about the Barnes visit: Jerry's legs had continued weakening since he fell in the garden. Surprised, I watched him nearly sprint from room to room, feasting on Picassos, Monets, and Soutines. On that day, he reminded me of our early, excited walks through galleries in Europe. For years afterward I would remember him gazing at a still life painting by Cézanne. Some apples on a table were still, as Jerry would be in years to come, resigned to a wheelchair. At the same time, the apples were created to have an inward motion, as though building strength to fly, whirl in the air, and leap off their tilted table. I don't know if Jerry thought of his coming immobility—his own loss of outward motion—but I'm glad we had that moment in Merion.

13

THE TURNING POINT

Tap, slide, tap, tap. I heard the Morse code's dots and dashes in the tapping of Jerry's aluminum cane on the road by our country house. He couldn't sleep, and had gone for an early walk that morning. His stiffness had increased, and the rod kept him from falling.

At the time, he was nervously aware of his limitations. It was in September, 1999, and we'd be leaving soon to celebrate our fortieth anniversary in London. That trip would be the turning point, the place clearly indicating what we had done once and could do no longer. Unlike our earlier impulsiveness, we booked a reservation, this time at the more expensive Savoy. Uneasy though he was, his jollity remained. "It takes a pragmatist to do whatever works," he joked, about using a leather-like toiletry pouch, given as a favor on a Concorde flight, for his multi-colored heart pills. He repeated it when purchasing a new cane at James Smith & Sons, where we'd once bought a Burberry umbrella.

On the Strand we affected Edwardian accents, jocularly speaking of Wilde and Gilbert and Sullivan as though they were close acquaintances. We saw Shakespeare at the Globe with tickets we could never have afforded on earlier forays. We reviewed the day's adventures over wines and dinners. At the National Gallery, we bought a postcard of Claude Monet's *Houses of Parliament* and placed it below our window at the Savoy, overlooking the same scene. On the TV we followed the news of John F. Kennedy Jr.'s plane crash, both saddened by the same thought: he would never have a long love like ours.

But nights were another thing. We spoke of the past, of our wedding trip when we walked full days for contact with the earth. Of later trips to France where once we stood on the street in a rainstorm, the sky salmon under shag clouds, watching trees bend over. We talked of running into the sea on Fire Island, and of walking from Washington Square Park down to the Hudson River, ticking off the historic houses on Greenwich Village side streets. Life had lowered the bar, but we marveled at its earlier height.

Shortly after the London trip, what he'd called a backache became nearly unbearable. Once, probably because of pain medication, he fainted on the street and was hospitalized for a bruised face and a fractured rib. The diagnosis was spinal stenosis, a condition in which the spinal column narrows and pinches the nerves. It was confirmed by extensive X-rays, bone scans, and CT scans. After attempts to keep the pain at bay, including caudal injections, physical therapy, massage, and even acupuncture, Jerry underwent a simple laminectomy to remove spinal plaque.

For the first weeks after surgery we expected a new life.

One day while he healed we walked, no, stumbled, the length of road that jutted out from a bay near our house in Springs. That beautiful headland was unbeautifully named Louse Point. Nodding back at the nodding beach roses, he looked longingly at a green island across the bay, as though he might trudge through water to reach it. I was hopeful. To be alive is to stumble, I thought. A statue stands upright, we do not.

But then, within weeks, a crippling spinal stenosis set in. His temper flared unaccountably at times, from shouts of "Where's my muffler?" to a tongue-clicking sound meaning I'd made a wrong turn while driving. His silences lengthened.

He was relegated first to a walker, and then to a wheelchair, but he often declined their use. Jerry had never been one to sit patiently. He had leaped, he had glided, he had run into freezing waves. He'd lose balance and fall and, at six feet two inches, he went down like an elm tree. Once he hit the floor and cracked a rib after merely reaching for a cutting board to prepare a fruit compote, an accompaniment for swordfish. A strong man, he was uneasy with his own disability. He concealed his anger when he had to be helped to his feet. As a doctor, he had been the healer, not the healed. If faith eases suffering, he was a sufferer, since he believed only in science. The surgeon's skill. Physical therapy. The medications he had to take every night, every morning. He did believe in life under any circumstances, at whatever cost.

What's more, when he fell he could not scramble to his feet. My arms were helpless to budge his two hundred pounds. One night he had to lie on the damp ground outside the house in Springs for hours until help arrived. I was angry that he could not walk and never would again, furious that I could not help him. Whom to fight? God, I supposed, resenting Yahweh's elusiveness. I tried to hide this storm, especially with students. Indeed I tried so hard that I bent the other way and allowed some failures to get by.

Wisdom informs us that body and mind are one, but my husband belied that proposition. For forty-five years an MD-virologist at Mount Sinai, he knew influenza's courses, and also what I could do for a muscle strain. He listed the causes of his own condition, some with their Latin names. He said "I don't know" more often than before, but that was for the good: illness had lessened his certainties, and increased his low-key humor.

Throughout our marriage both of us worked as professors. While I continued teaching, his position at Mount Sinai was threatened. In 2006, he was forced to resign because of their budget: his salary could support two or more young scientists in his department. After grumbling in outrage, he made peace with the departmental decision. He would retire, to read novels and listen to music. A favorite distraction was the sudoku, just as the crossword puzzle had been a generation before. He'd fill in blank spaces as though he were trying a new virus experiment.

"Why do you do it?" I asked once.

"To know the mind can discover logic by filling in the blanks."

"But there is no logic in the world," I protested.

"Yes, there is," he replied, and I felt his conviction.

However, he spoke less about his achievements, as though his scientific discoveries were consigned to a past life. At times

I thought, Well, that was a fine life, his past better than most lives of the present. At other times I lamented that his physical condition was progressive. While his mind was intact, he was slower to respond.

Five years before his retirement, my own life had taken a different turn. I'd found myself writing poems with increasing intensity. While comforting Jerry, keeping house, and teaching, I wrote new lines with wonder and delight, discovering a part of myself I hadn't known before. One day in 2000, the phone rang. It was Pat Strachan, senior editor at Houghton Mifflin, saying she wanted to schedule my fourth book of poems, *The Paintings of Our Lives*, for publication a year later. In the book is a psalm to our long marriage—to the recurrences, the ruptures healed. Set on the roof of our city building at sunset, the poem ends:

> Praise to the sun
> that flares and flares again in fierce explosions
> even after sunset, to muddy rivers
> that glow vermillion now, to second chances.

I was thrilled when Pat, who had once been Derek Walcott's editor, accepted *Paintings*, and guided into print my *Days of Wonder: New and Selected Poems*, which appeared in 2002. One year after that, in 2003, came my edition of *The Poems of Marianne Moore*, which her literary estate had asked me to prepare. It made available to readers poems she had excluded from her own so-called complete edition, or nearly half her work.

The good news was also frightening when I remembered,

early in our marriage, that Jerry had found his career while I was still floundering. My sense of failure had wounded him. Now my work was read while Jerry was on the downside of his accomplishments. And he was more generous that I'd been, unfazed by the redress of balance, continually nudging me on.

About the edition, I was glad to be of service to Marianne Moore's readers. But Jerry had expressed concern: "Get back to your own poems. That's what she would say." I did, with fervor. Unlike anything else I've done, writing poetry gives me the chance to strive for an ideal Marianne Moore called "the genuine," and to know what William Carlos Williams meant when he declared, "Only the imagination is real!" Though Pat left the company, Houghton published another two books of mine, and still counting. Jerry's gladness was pure. When I thought of my discontent early in our marriage, how I wished I'd had Jerry's largeness.

14

MOON SHELL

Jerry's decline was long and steady. I pushed the wheel-chair to neighborhood restaurants. We went to see every Shakespeare production we could find, notably *Twelfth Night* and the *Richard III* with Mark Rylance. We heard James Galway play Mozart's Flute Concerto and marveled at his long, sweeping phrases, his staccato notes. We visited old friends. We went to see new acquaintances, phoning ahead with the all-purpose question "Wheelchair accessible?" Once, when we were on our way to a party, four young men lifted him and his chair up the steps, through the door, and, later, home again, as they drank Sancerre all the way. All four remarked on his unflagging dignity.

It was never a fine morning when I would enter the shed in back of our house and see our two well-used bikes in extra tall sizes, bikes we'd found that would fit our elongated bodies. In greener days, when we'd set out for the promontory nearby,

Jerry fairly flew, and it was work to catch up with him. When his legs buckled and he lost balance, his bike leaned on its rack in the shed, the tires flat. We kept it there, unable to let it go.

Paradoxically, my freest moments also became grim reminders of what was and what had been. When I ran down to the seashore at the time of the summer solstice, the silvery light stayed until nearly nine o'clock. The sand was pocked with footprints. Could I have seen Jerry's running shoes imprinted there? My mind went back to days when he had dived into breakers, or into bay water to swim alongside cormorants, his lean, active body moving to express the emotions he so often hid in his speech.

In the twin wish to be independent and to hold fast to Jerry, I told others of *our* illness—*our* orthopedist, *our* wheelchair confinement. I could not disjoin us. At first, I wanted to feel his back pain, to know what it was like. Then one night I reeled in soreness, certain that I did feel it. We were separate, distinctly different, yet fused in the binding of two souls.

Often Marianne Moore's words come back to me: "Don't relive desperate situations or anticipate others. If you follow that rule, half of life's problems will vanish." I've tried to practice that advice, assessing what any given moment can offer. And for us there was bounty in the moment: animated conversations, grilled dinners in Springs with friends. When the waves of Schubert's Impromptus rose to the cathedral ceilings of our house I felt certain there was no other peace like ours.

Unable to speak, even to Jerry, of the wholeness I felt, I wrote "Moon Shell":

August, I walk this shore in search of wholeness
among snapped razor clams and footless quahogs.
How easily my palm cradles a moon shell

coughed up on shore. I stroke the fragments
as, last night, I stroked your arm
smelling of salt, scrubbed clean by the sea air.

Once you loped near me. Now, in my mind's eye,
your rubbery footsoles track sand hills
the shape of waves you no longer straddle.

You inch forward, step, comma, pause,
your silences the wordless rage of pain.
But still at night our bodies merge in sleep

and fit unbroken, like the one perfect shell
I've never found and can only imagine—
and crack when we're apart. I clutch the moon shell,

guardian of unknowing, chipped and silent,
until I fling it down and feel its loss.
Broken, it fit my hand and I was whole.

Jerry's infirmity made it impermissible for me to be sick.
In my seventies, the odds were that my own health could fail,
but I waved away them away. Then, in 2012, my sabbatical
year, I broke my ankle falling from a bike. That morning, I
had walked to the shed of our country house, glanced guiltily
at his abandoned bike, and mounted my own, bound for the
promontory at Gerard Park. I passed wildflowers, blue chicory,
sea lavender, scrub roses, and the starry weeds the locals call

bedstraw. I marveled at the landscape, and I thought how the early settlers had gypped Wyandanch, the Montauk sachem, when they bought his land for knives, mirrors, overcoats, and a machine for husking corn. Ahead of me was the bay, spangled water in the early morning sun. This was my first ride of the season, and in the thrill of it I didn't notice, under my wheels, fallen branches and cracked clamshells on the blacktop. Suddenly, the balance lost, the parabolic curve through air.

Too stunned for the full pain to set in, and having forgotten my cell phone, I biked back to the house and limped up the drive, my ankle by then grown to the size of an apple. Later, when the ambulance driver told me I must be in pain, I felt it rise and bloom. Then the X-ray image that looked like white smoke. The malleolus bone was cracked; my left hand, too, was fractured, and the orthopedist's sentence was to stay off the foot for six weeks or make it worse. And worse I could not afford to risk.

Indeed, I was fortunate in having the sabbatical, or fellowship leave, as it was called at Baruch. I lay in bed with a laptop computer and finished a book of poems, *Without a Claim*, which I could do with my pointer fingers. Jerry's response was kind, though impractical. At first, when I had staggered to the house, he had denied the ankle was broken, and was slow to call an ambulance. "A bad sprain," he said, fetching ice. At the hospital he became agitated, read the X-ray, and frowned. He winced when the orthopedist immobilized my whole leg in a hip-high CAM boot. Though he said nothing, I'd seen him grimace before, at times when he refrained from crying out against inappropriate medical care. It was only a boot, after all. Later that day, he stuffed me into his car and drove us to New

York, swearing that he could take care of me.

Our marriage had certainly survived reversals. Earlier it was the crossing of our careers. In illness, Jerry had been caregiver to me and my family; now I was "It." And Jerry saw in my accident another change of roles. He would help me recover. But this time it didn't work. He brought dinner plates that slipped off his walker, and he fell while helping me bathe. Within a few days, we hired a home-care aide to assist us both.

Jerry's incorrect diagnosis of the fracture illustrates why many doctors are reluctant to treat their families. He wanted so much to believe nothing was wrong that he made it so in his mind. Deep down, he knew he was mistaken. Many years before, I'd fallen off a bike at Yaddo, causing only a bruised hip bone. A fellow visitor, a surgeon who wrote novels, told me my hip was injured but not fractured. When I phoned Jerry, he said wittily, "A surgeon without an X-ray machine has only a novelist's impression of whether your hip is broken." And he ordered, "Call a taxi bound for the nearest hospital." Not so when I broke my ankle in 2012.

It was a three-hour motor trip to our country house, and now I was the driver. Jerry had been forced to turn away from the cars he'd relished since his early Austin-Healey. The last time Jerry drove, we were both in danger. The paralysis, along with a creeping case of peripheral neuropathy, or nerve damage, had kept him from feeling his legs in space. On a road close to the house, he lost control of the car, went through a yield sign, and hit another car at a traffic circle. No one was injured. However, I was mending a broken foot, and I'd propped it up, in a CAM boot, my very long legs reaching the dashboard.

Had the impact been harder, my leg would have unhealed itself, at the very least. The other car's passengers came toward our car, which now was pulled over on the roadside. "Couldn't you come to see if we were injured?" one of them asked. Then, noticing Jerry's disorientation and my booted leg, she withdrew. We called the police and reported the accident. Soon after, we visited Jerry's neurologist, who, examining him, exclaimed, "Why on earth are you still driving?" That did it. Jerry sold his Lexus, the last descendant of the cars that had delighted him. By now Jerry burned with losses, the absence of control, the ban on motoring. I, who had kept a Honda in the city throughout our separation and reunion, regretted losing the freedom of driving alone on the highway. Yet I was glad of the opportunity to deliver my husband from his chair in the closed-in apartment to the country house, and to be alone in the car with him, talking of weekend plans or of the weekend just past, listening to music. So it went, the mixed bag of our marriage opening for me and spilling out joys and losses. Weighing them was useless. Life just was. Is.

The years of Jerry's pain also offered moments of intense joy which were heightened by an awareness of life's temporality. Then, in 2014, Jerry's dizziness and imbalance forecast a second stroke, the first having been in 2000, heralded by a loss of vision, the condition called amaurosis fugax. It had caused some paralysis but had allowed him to go on with his life. The new symptoms occurred just in time for him to have surgery on his one remaining, failing carotid artery (his other had closed long before). The successful operation was followed by three other procedures, all in one year. The first two terrified me, but

did not faze him: they consisted of surgery for three poten-
tially killing aneurisms, then angioplasty for yet another heart
attack. The third, he confessed, was painful: for the heart's
"low ejection fraction," or the reduced percentage of blood
leaving the heart when it contracts, an implanted defibrillator
had to be inserted lest his heart, deprived of oxygen, went into
fibrillation. I shuddered when one of his several cardiologists
tried to ease my fears by telling me Jerry would be all right for
what the doctor called "the short term."

Religion was of little help to me in waiting areas, but at
times I succumbed. During my vigils in the hospital, I prayed
in the Interfaith Chapel at Mount Sinai. It was a large room, as
neutral in appearance as its name, with a large abstract painting for an altar, as if to remind the visitor of its religious objec-
tivity. He is God's servant, I mumbled. He has worked to save
lives. I smiled at two Muslim men who prostrated themselves
on the floor, and again at a woman fingering beads. I warmed
to a young woman's knowing glance as she sat on the bench in
front of mine. I was numb. All of those life-or-death procedures
had overwhelmed me. In moments of clarity, I wondered if
they could save him. But they did. After each of his surgeries I
left the chapel to rejoice that the operation had succeeded.

When Jerry could no longer walk from room to room, I realized my limitations and hired professional helpers for him. As
time passed, the noise level rose in our one-bedroom apartment
and the walls rang with the voices of home-care aides, physical therapists, occupational therapists, and visiting nurses.
Although I enjoyed Jerry's company whatever his condition,
I soon preferred staying in my college office longer than I had

to, seated at a gray metallic desk. With my door closed, I could be alone to work.

My role as caregiver demanded management of his meals, his hygiene schedule, the doctors' visits, the therapists' visits, and preparation for sleep. Nightly, I placed in his hand the electric massager and the vibrator prescribed for his back pain and lifted the bedrails to keep him from rolling off the mattress. The chores comforted me in the face of larger worries, such as the danger that resulted from his resistance to the confinement. It took two bloody accidents for Jerry to agree to the bedrails. "I won't fall off the bed," he snapped when at first I proposed it. After the first drop, I attempted grim humor, saying I disliked seeing bloodstains on the carpet. When humor failed, I tried commands, then threats. Finally he accepted the metal nighttime cage, and soon said he was grateful that I'd insisted. He showed quieter resignation later, when two additional fences were required, one at the head and one at the foot, to keep him from climbing out in his sleep.

And I held him at night, all night whenever his body could bear the pressure of my body touching his. Seeking the parts of him that were not in pain, I reached across his waist and stroked his belly.

In the years of Jerry's illness, some moments were unnecessarily fraught, making me wish later that I had a less compulsive, more Zenned-out persona. I'd panic when a tardy home-care aide kept me from meeting a class on time. I'd shout demotic four-letter curses when, waiting on a street corner, we'd see an unoccupied yellow cab ride past, its driver unlawfully declining the bother of taking us with the wheelchair. Other moments, though, were serious warnings, and I couldn't always make a quick distinction between the two.

One frightening spell was Hurricane Sandy, the storm whose ravaging effects lasted one week for us, longer for many others, and during which I first realized that the word "power" meant not political one-upmanship but instead no phone—not even the landline—and no light, no heat, no Internet connection, no water, no working fridge. We lived on the fourteenth floor, and our neighborhood was among the most damaged. Flooding had caused an explosion in a power plant not far away, and from our windows no lights could be seen in that usually luminous part of town. Claustrophobia prevailed. The few cars on the road, presumably in desperation, careered around without traffic lights. Our building's stairwell was Stygian, hard to navigate, and we had no flashlight. I did, however, walk down and up the steep flights carrying water and what canned food supplies I could find.

Not all hours were dark: On the gas stove, which still flamed, I cooked the canned-tuna casseroles I used to put together in our early days together. We read by candlelight and listened to music and news on a portable radio. I could walk to an N.Y.U. building, several blocks away, whose officials had offered neighbors power for their computers. But all week my body was tense with fear. Even if we'd been invited to sleep uptown, where people apparently still had power, there would have been no way to carry Jerry from our fourteenth-floor apartment. In case of a heart attack, I imagined running for help; an ambulance might come and a stretcher could bump him down the fourteen flights in time to avert tragedy. After what had come to seem years, the lights went back on and the water began to flow. We uttered the kind of wordless,

joyful cries I thought must have been heard on the first day
of Creation.

In time, our one-bedroom apartment came to look like the
storage room of an orthopedic ward. Tucked behind an arm-
chair were canes, a transport wheelchair I pushed, and a board
for Jerry's balance exercises. Two walkers, one a rollator, stood
next to his chair in the dining area. In the bedroom was a sta-
tionary bike he'd ridden before his legs failed. At the country
house, we had a ramp built over the front steps, but it proved
too steep for me to push Jerry's weight uphill, and I feared that
rolling downhill might plunge him into the pine trees. For a
time, on foot and with help, he was able to shamble into the
house, and "for a time" described just about every action in
our lives.

A motorized wheelchair was a test of our sanguineness.
It began with enthusiasm. Our friends, the writers Jan Heller
Levi and Christophe Keller, helped us select one. Christophe,
as a young man, had been paralyzed from an accident, and he
suggested we buy one like his, from Numotion, which cost
us only a hundred dollars after group health insurance paid.
However, it took months to receive it: there were appointments for measurements; physicians' letters, sent sometimes
repeatedly; insurance regulations and forms. Disagreements
arose: I felt it would be dangerous for Jerry to leave the house
unaccompanied, while he envisioned its allowing him to travel
alone to do neighborhood chores. I adjured him to value what
he had—his sharp mind, his sensibility to music and painting,
his affectionate home. He wanted more. From taxis he looked
longingly at the pavements he knew. When we drove to the

bays, city or country, he gazed at the water with a lover's intensity, and the sadness of a lover rebuffed. When I left him with an aide to teach or give a reading, or simply to walk on the sidewalks or the dunes, Jerry would live vicariously in my outings, however brief, and eagerly ask for details. Still, the joys balanced things out: his eyes twinkled when he watched a sunset or read aloud a passage from a book he wanted to share with me. His smile broadened when our nephew, David Schulman, Edward's son, brought over a homemade chocolate-caramel candy which we'd feast on for days and then wangle for more.

Jerry was crafty at hiding, even from himself, the gravity of his illness. That skill, famously called denial, had obvious drawbacks, but did offer a way of going on. Although he knew that his heart was pumping at a small fraction of the minimum, Jerry phoned in February of what would be his fatal year for tickets to see a new play at the Brooklyn Academy of Music the following autumn. He ordered new novels online, and bought tailored, no-iron chinos for the following summer.

I continued working, thanks to a sequence of home-care aides, some of them sent by the Visiting Nurse Service of New York. When it became clear that Jerry required full-time care, we succeeded in hiring Velma Duffus, who had been a companion to our beloved painter, Hedda Sterne, until she died. Velma, who was steady, sensitive, and devoted, tended Jerry during the day, while two nighttime attendants lifted him from bed to bath table. The two were Adam Iddrissu and Nana Kyei Baaluor, who spelled each other through the night.

Fortunately, Jerry liked them. He was a chooser. He retained a knifelike acuity, and a sage perception about people and things, which made it possible for me to forget for occasional moments that he was gravely ill. On one of the last days of his life, I printed for him the draft of a new poem, as I had habitually done for years, and he read it slowly with a single astute comment: "It's good, but not your best."

Early in April 2016, on the night of a beautiful day, Jerry writhed and uttered, "The pain is unbearable. It's more than I can stand." Hearing him in the kitchen, I turned off the stove, gave him the second of his daily pain pills, plugged in his electric massager and reached for his vibrator. No relief. I massaged his thigh, clumsily, reciting a Navajo night chant I remembered:

> O god of the silver water,
> god of the night sky,
> come flying over my house
> past the dark cloud,
> restore my body
> and let me walk with you.

15

FACING IT

One day, early in 2016, I asked if he wanted to be driven to one of the bays near our country house. He lay back in bed and said: "You have to understand that I have advanced cardiac failure." I assumed that he was addressing his own denial, as well as mine, but I took his words to heart, and went out for air. Ella Specht, one of his aides on Long Island, had come in with her "Hello, handsome." To soften his words that had started to pound in my head, I walked down the road to an inlet on the Sound called Fireplace Bay. It was so named because fire was, historically, communication: the Indians had lighted fires there to warn of danger. Later, the settlers had thrown seaweed over fire for smoke-clouds that would tell islanders across the bay that food was on its way. At that moment, I stood gazing at the seemingly endless sky, wishing that life could be unceasing. *Advanced cardiac failure. Insufficient heart function.* I longed for the fire-speech that would blaze up and shout: no, don't leave, stay, linger.

All that year I wished for a twig or a plume or a magic root
to heal my husband, a rod or a wizard's tea to lift his suffering. Where science shrugged, there had to be a stone, a dung
beetle, a paste of flowers, that could cure. We shared so much
it again seemed wrong that I could not feel his agony. Next day
he was unresponsive, even when I told him of a lecture I'd just
heard by Peter Sellars, who had directed a version we'd seen
of Bach's *St. Matthew Passion*, conducted by Simon Rattle, at
the Park Avenue Armory eight months before. We'd lauded his
performance—actually a rehearsal, since we couldn't get tickets. In his talk, Sellars repeated his instructions to the cast: "Go
to your place of deepest hurt and perform from there. Use the
crisis as invitation." Disaster as opportunity was what I learned
from his command, and I was to remember it in the weeks and
months ahead.

Alix Kates Shulman has written of the power of crisis in
her book, *To Love What Is*, about the challenges in caring
for a brain-injured husband. The title is a rough translation
of Nietzsche's *amor fati*—to embrace, not simply accept, all
events, however painful. And Joseph Campbell goes further in
urging us to bring love, not discouragement, to adversity, and
thereby derive strength.

On the day when he reminded us both of his cardiac failure, Jerry's impassiveness had differed from his usual silences.
When I probed, he had not been able to speak, so great was the
pain, so groggy was he from inability to sleep the night before.
I lay in bed with him, holding him around the waist all that
night. Or was it more than one night? Time was losing its reli-
ability. Pain fools with time. It stretches a minute into an hour
or contracts a full day into a minute.

After the confrontation came hospital stays, more blood-pressure drops; medication changes, repeated visits to cardiologists, blood-pressure specialists, electro-cardiologists; defibrillator checks. On April 21, magically he pulled himself together for a ceremony celebrating an honor I received, the Frost Medal for Distinguished Lifetime Achievement in American Poetry. For him it was a payback for all the rejection letters he had intercepted to spare me; the coaching he had done; for the pep talks; for the belief. When, in January, the phone call had come from Ruth Kaplan, president of the Poetry Society of America (PSA), which presented the award, Jerry announced that he would stay alive long enough to attend the event. And he did.

After that, he'd wake mornings to ask if I'd written my Frost Medal lecture, and could he see what I'd done. And did I remember to invite this person or that.

Jerry smiled when he read William Merwin's letter to me.

"Your Frost award, long overdue, takes me back to the days when you fell over handlebars," William wrote, referring to my numerous spills from bikes. Then he looked closer. William's vision had been failing, and his letters were typed—but with handwritten corrections, the pen strokes seemingly put down by faith he would not miss the page.

Jerry dispatched our nephew, David, to have orchids sent to me, Alice Quinn, and Kimiko Hahn, two officers of the PSA who would be there. He arrived in his wheelchair accompanied by Velma Duffus and grandly greeted well-wishers.

One week after the Frost occasion, a sudden downturn. His internist admitted him to Mount Sinai hospital for observation. An examination had revealed anemia, abnormally low blood pressure, evidence in stool of internal bleeding, and heartbeat arrhythmia. After several further tests and some adjustments of medications, he was discharged to the home care of the Mobile Acute Care Team, or MACT, the hospital's program for severely ill patients. So grew another surge of caring professionals, doctors, nurses, more physical and occupational therapists. Often they disagreed. One physical therapist believed Jerry should try to stand and walk; another wanted to keep him comfortable through massage and stretching. There were visits from health-care workers who had become his friends, such as Gaetano Lombardo and Shou-An Liu, from Academy Physical Therapy. For years, with unflagging patience, they had treated his spinal stenosis, and now I could see the look of palliative resignation on their faces.

In that circus-like atmosphere, duties increased for our staple health-care workers, Velma, Adam, and Nana. Over the past year, Jerry had sometimes been incontinent, and now, when it worsened, I ordered boxes of chucks, diapers, disposable boxer shorts, and dry pads for bed and chairs. The four of us pretended to minimize the sanitary measures in the hope of lessening his humiliation. When his incontinence was rampant, I would hold Jerry in my arms until he fell asleep, then make up the couch for myself in the living room. June brought hot nights, and our only AC was in the bedroom. When I couldn't sleep, I silently repeated a shibboleth from my father, that resting in the dark is the same as sleeping. Not true, but quieting.

Velma became indispensable. Whenever she wasn't cleaning him, walking him when he could walk, taking him to doctors' appointments, she read books from our library and joined us in merry talk at the lunch table. When he could no longer rise to his feet, she coaxed the last drop of mobility from him by helping him to limp to his wheelchair or walker. "I can't *stand*," he would complain bitterly. "Yes, you can," she flashed back at him.

Adam and Nana came to our rescue when Jerry had to be lifted and carried to bath and table. Adam stood a head taller than even Jerry and I, and could lift Jerry's two hundred pounds as if he were fluffing a pillow. Remarkably, his weight-lifting of Jerry occurred while he was fasting during the Muslim holiday of Ramadan. While I sincerely meant my "Ramadan Mubarak" blessing for him, I was concerned: June turned out to be the last, and most agonizing, month of Jerry's life. Usually Adam slept on a recliner in our bedroom, alert for Jerry's call. Sometimes he left but would drive back within minutes of my summoning. One night, Adam arrived with food, and asked to use the microwave at 3 a.m., when his religious precepts allowed him to break his Ramadan fast. I said no as I lay on the couch near the kitchen, trying desperately for an hour of sleep. He accepted my apology, but kept me awake asking repeatedly where he could find things he needed for Jerry's care.

Our helpers were crucial, but I wanted to do personally what caregiving I could. Although I'd be gone to give lectures occasionally, I'd spend no more than a few hours away and return in good time to supervise the aides. One day a letter came from Alfred Corn, with whom I had recently served on a poetics panel.

Dear Grace,
I know this is a risk but I will say that your frailty
has me very, very worried. There was a visible
decline since the Frost Medal evening. Grace, you
aren't a wrestling champion. This present situation
can't continue. If your health worsens and you
become invalided, what then will Jerry do? You
must rest. There is a limit to everything and that
includes selflessness. You have reached it now. Please
authorize yourself to care for your own well-being.
And please forgive this sternness, which is only a
side product of Love, Alfred

My caregiving, I felt, was not selfless. It provided a close-
ness I'd never had with anyone. It awakened compassion,
opening my heart to the sufferings of another. I was able to
empathize with others who were afflicted, such as an auditor in
my Great Works class at Baruch, a man who navigated a walker
into elevators and through crowds to read the classics. At
the same time, I was exhausted. I wish now that I could have
hidden my sleep deprivation from Jerry. It was dizzying, and
it interfered with daily tasks. He knew, though. Once when I
told him that I enjoyed ministering to him, he cut through the
froth with "I'm a pain in the ass." Wanting to keep that candor
between us, I replied, "Yes, but you're *my* pain in the ass." His
blank expression told me that he didn't understand, beneath
my banter, the importance caregiving had for me: it enabled
me to feel deeply the oneness of our two separate selves, and
consequently the depth of our love.

16

THE FALL

Jerry's cardiologist, Herschel Sklaroff, was on the phone with me every day, checking on blood pressures after adjusting medications, cutting down on Lasix and Coreg. He taught me the exact dosages for morning and evening. I fed the pills fearfully, knowing that exactness in dispensing medicine was not my forte, but Dr. Sklaroff assured me that Jerry was doing well. On June 30, he ordered an office visit, sick as the patient was, explaining that he couldn't practice medicine only on the phone. Outside the bare-walled room where Jerry lay on the examining table, the doctor said to me, "Stage four. Advanced cardiac failure. He's a very sick man. I've done all I can."

Wisely, Dr. Sklaroff decided against putting him in the hospital, because it could not help. "I have faith," I said to the doctor, trying hard to believe my own words. I was relieved by the doctor's judgment. I wanted Jerry home, even though I'd been coping with a new challenge every day. Once, at

sunrise, I found him lying on the floor. He had climbed over
three bedrails in his sleep, as though wanting to get out of his
aching body. His overnight aides were changing guard. Sadly,
I'd heard him from the couch calling "Velma. Adam. Nana."
None came. From the time I found him, I kept phoning in
desperation, but it was hours before one of them arrived to
lift him back into bed. The night doorman sheepishly refused
to help, for legal reasons. During that terrible time, I tried to
move him and he didn't budge. Finally, Nana arrived. "Prince!"
Jerry called out. Sometimes he addressed him that way. He
explained that Nana was a man's name in Ghana, a title often
used for male royalty. At other times he called Nana "Seth"
after Adam and Eve's third son, who was said to be virtuous
and wise. That morning, after Jerry was safe, I adjured him to
stay put. I knew I meant stay alive, already feeling the disconnect between us. I was losing him.

I cherish the gift of his last days at home. Often he was
disoriented, at midnight calling for his dress shoes "to go to
the opera," and saying, once, his hazel eyes unfocused, "I have
marshmallows in my socks." I was amazed that such confusion
hadn't happened before, considering his heart's failure to pump
oxygen to his brain. Being at home offered him familiar things,
his iPad, his music on the powerful speakers he'd built, his
own pillows, the sights and sounds and smells of all he wanted
to live for. And the days shimmered with affection. The cut
off came dramatically one night when, in a split second, he
changed. His face was now expressionless. His eyes were
vague. I'd implored, questioned, and then dissolved in tears.

Thursday, June 30. The visit to Dr. Sklaroff occurred
on the final day of Jerry's life. A concert was to be his last

memory: as an Army captain in Salzburg when he had heard
Mozart's "Jupiter" Symphony for the first time. He was transported, his fellow officer restless. How music takes us full
circle, I thought, thankful that I had been his "Jupiter" companion in later years.

At 5 p.m., when we returned from Dr. Sklaroff's office, he
rested in the recliner I use as a desk chair. Trying to lighten the
gloom, I did a three-bears routine with "Who's been sitting in
my chair?" He stared. I took his hand. "Do you know me?" I
said. "Liebchen Grace," he replied, pressing my hand. A pause,
then he uttered with clarity: "I love you *so much.*" I kissed his
temple, and overcome, I went out to the park for air and an ice-
cream cone, an outlet that replaced the cigarette habit I'd given
up years before. I stopped by the fountain where we met. No
guitar players were visible. Nearby, a musician who somehow
wheeled a grand piano onto a concrete path played a Mozart
concerto we'd heard together at Lincoln Center. The music
was elevating—even the flat notes—because it had brought
us together. In half an hour I returned to find Jerry tearing off
his shirt and pleading to be left alone in a thin voice I did not
recognize.

That evening I watched Jerry fall. Seeing him on the bathroom floor, I asked Nana, who was on then, to lift him to our
bed. Nana had filled the tub, preparing to bathe him. He knelt
by Jerry's shoulder and, looking up, shook his head, lowered
his eyes, and commanded, "Call an ambulance." I did, and
waited by Jerry's side.

Still I didn't believe it was over. How could it be—this
magnitude, this bounty, this joy? Yes, it could be the end, I
realized, when I remembered, some days before the turning,

that he held my face in both hands and cried out, "God help me. God help us both. If there is a God." It was the first time in all our years together that he had said "God." Then he said, "Promise me never to leave my side." I never did.

We would not speak again. The EMS personnel took over, examined him, and asked for his living will. I'd kept it with mine, in a file folder marked "Death." Without his signed DNR ("do not resuscitate"), he might have been revived brain-dead, and would have had to die twice. I didn't watch as they lifted him onto a gurney, pounded his chest, breathed into his mouth, and did whatever else they could to revive him. "We have honored his wishes," the EMS doctor said at last, then reached out a hand to steady me as I lurched forward. Jerry was dead.

In an effort to clear the haze, I draw details from documents and from memory. In doing so, I suspect that our actions that day were more awkward, less purposeful, than these words can convey. There were things left unsaid, disruption, confusion. The EMS certificate gives the time of Jerry's death as 6:20 p.m. I remember a medical examiner phoning the cardiologist to record cardiac insufficiency. During those last weeks I had kept reality at bay, hoping he might rise again. Now I would walk through the fire. I thought of how the medics had left him lying on the living room floor. Of how I had looked at his face, which was neither at peace nor contorted in pain. Distressed, perhaps. Surprised. He knew the severity of his illness, but wanted—no, expected—to live. A round-faced police officer, called by the EMS, asked permission to remove Jerry's watch and wedding ring. I slipped the band on my ring finger and felt married to him yet again. Repeatedly I said to him, "I love you *so* much," believing that hearing was the last sense to go. I covered him with a blanket because I remembered how, months before, he had shivered in a cold spring. I kissed his lips and stroked his still-warm belly, and I stayed with him until the chapel workers came. I would have stayed on then, too, but the officer ushered me into the bedroom while two strangers carried him away.

I am alive and incomplete, my future unknown. Jerry is complete and perfect, unalterable. No more will medications help his heart, electric massagers soothe his legs, or my hands console him.

The dirge from Shakespeare's *Cymbeline* was going through my head:

> Fear no more the heat o' the sun,
> Nor the furious winter's rages;
> Thou thy worldly task hast done,
> Home art gone, and ta'en thy wages·
> Golden girls and lads all must,
> As chimney-sweepers, come to dust.

My emotions were chaotic. I wished that the medics had taken him to our bed, where we'd made love for half a century, so that I could massage his thighs once more. I sobbed, then stiffened in anger. When he'd exacted from me the promise never to leave his side, I asked if he'd ever leave mine. "Never," he pledged. But he left. It would be days before the sorrow would move in over the anger, a dense fog after a storm.

I wanted not to sit shiva. My preference disconcerted friends of various creeds who followed the custom of bringing food to the bereaved. That was not for me. On the night Jerry died, after I phoned our nephew David, my shaken words barely decipherable, my friends Susan Shapiro and Charlie Rubin, who live nearby, took me to dinner at Knickerbocker's, a restaurant on University Place. On the following day, aimlessly walking through Washington Square Park, I ran into two of my undergraduate poetry students, Benjamin Long and Andrew "Pooka" Paik, who had come from uptown to see the neighborhood. I told them Jerry had died the night before, and showed them the "singing" fountain where Jerry and I first met. Later, both of them wrote poems about accidentally finding me there. Ben's was "By the Fountain":

> And there you left us to our days,
> Parked on a plinth, three became two,

and Pooka's referred to the Scotch-Irish ballad I sang when Jerry and I first met:

> Sorrow, sing sorrow
> Sing in a fountain
> Where a cloud sails by
> Like a milk-white steed.

I was moved to nothing less than belief in an afterlife when six of my students presented me with a little book, whose covers they had sewn by hand. It contained poems each of them had composed for Jerry. On its back page, they had written:

> For Grace and Jerome, for all our souls, with love
> and friendship, from Pooka, Ben, Sarah, Ashley, Susan,
> and Kyah.

Friends indulged me in my wish to meet them outside the home where Jerry died. Meena Alexander walked with me in Washington Square Park. Eating ice creams we bought from a stand, we listened to the current musicians, a piano and a sax, both a far cry from the guitar-carrying folksingers of yesteryear. Benjamin Taylor took me to dinner at Sapphire, an Indian restaurant uptown that the three of us had visited. We spoke not a word of grief, instead talked animatedly of Edmund Gosse's *Father and Son*; of Ben's new manuscript, a memoir that became *The Hue and Cry at Our House: A Year Remembered*; and of people we knew.

Richard Howard and his husband, David Alexander, took me to our neighborhood restaurant, North Square, and again no word was said of grief. I liked that. The conversation, filled with stimulating cultural events, emphasized life, not death, and acknowledged that there was no consolation.

At home, I looked in the mirror and did not recognize myself. I was suddenly old, not the young woman Jerry had me believing I was. "He will always be with you" was the well-meant phrase that rankled. In spirit, yes. But let's not minimize physicality. I wanted him more than "in my heart." I wanted his body. In his presence, a thousand things could happen. We could intuit each other's thoughts. To recapture that presence—and to avoid mirrors that reflected my change—I walked, walked, walked in the city, retracing his elongated footsteps that must be imprinted permanently in the street pavements and park roads.

In the apartment where he died, small things took on major importance. A pajama button, too late to sew back on; his satchel of heart medications—Coreg, Januvia, Lasix,

Flomax, Lipitor, Diovan—that could neither be used again nor tossed. His cards—nondriver ID, health insurance, credit, bank—that would remain in my wallet even when canceled. In his midnight-blue blazer pocket were torn ticket stubs to Mahler's Symphony No. 1 at the Philharmonic. The stubs and the blazer would stay in his closet, along with clothes, shoes, diplomas. I pressed to my ears the stethoscope from his early medical training, his name taped to one handle.

After notifying friends and family, I e-mailed the news of Jerry's death to his colleagues. Dr. Peter Palese, chair of microbiology at Mount Sinai, replied by sending me a copy of an announcement he had circulated among the faculty. Dr. Palese described Jerry as a pioneering virologist in influenza research, adding that most of the work in his field around the world "builds on his earlier findings."

He pointed to Jerry's discovery of animal models, now widely used, for influenza A and B viruses. To me he wrote: "Jerry's studies laid the groundwork for understanding the cellular arm of immune responses following infections, and was instrumental in opening up this new field of viral immunology." Peter Palese's own persistent work in the field, and his respect for the past, reminded me of how Jerry likened the scientific process to artistic labors. Peter was to say it in a few words: "Science is like throwing a stone—uphill. Nothing is easy."

An old friend, Dr. Rhonda Rosenberg, a research scientist at a southern university, sent me copies of their influenza papers, which I read with the zeal of a traveler learning the language of a brave new world.

My regrets multiplied. I had known that he discovered

the uniqueness of the Hong Kong virus, and of its widespread consequences. The finding would obviate disaster, since the virus had killed an estimated million people worldwide in 1968–69. I knew that his later studies had laid the groundwork for current understanding and prevention of the disease. As a young woman, I'd known about his subsequent work. Indeed I'd stretched my brain to read about his studies in immunity to influenza. I knew that he had fulfilled his wish to treat the many, rather than the few, by doing virus research instead of practicing medicine. However, I never knew the scope of his discoveries. I see now that it was either because of Jerry's blessed absence of egomania or my ignorance, or a combination of both. While he knew my poems well, and even in his last days read that draft I gave him, I'd been hard put to absorb the truth of his lifesaving work. Nevertheless, the facts of his achievement are out there rising in what I've come to believe to be Jerry's continuance, the ascent of his soul among Irving Howe's rose shrubs.

17

THE AFTERGLOW

At six o'clock on the day after Jerry died, I entered the Church of the Ascension at Tenth Street and Fifth Avenue, a few blocks from my home. Ascension is one of the two churches Henry James praised in 1904 as being too fine to escape demolition in a city of skyscrapers. They waited out that time, though, and in 1965 there came the Landmarks Commission which would save them.

Ascension is a nineteenth-century Gothic edifice among modern residential buildings. Episcopalian, it blessed some prominent American marriage ceremonies. Its look-alike, also delicate in brownstone, is the First Presbyterian Church at Twelfth Street and Fifth, where Marianne Moore's body had been on view.

I'd been to Ascension with Jerry for concerts conducted by Dennis Keene, glorious choral performances of the Fauré, Bach, and Mozart requiems. That was not why I sat in a central pew on the day after his death. Instead, it was to gaze at the mural of Christ's ascension, an altarpiece painted by John La Farge.

I'd fixed on that painting, its angels in pairs attired in blue, green, and violet robes singing the flight of Christ from the dead, lit by sun filtered through stained-glass windows. In that time and place, I didn't feel Jerry's presence. Concerts had stirred him, while houses of worship had not. But my visit was distracting. I'd read an odd fact about the mural in Christopher Benfey's book *The Great Wave: Gilded Age Misfits, Japanese Eccentrics, and the Opening of Old Japan.* Benfey writes that La Farge, commissioned to paint the mural and stuck for inspiration, had traveled to Japan and was awed by Mount Fuji. The backstory had changed my perception of the painting, blending a snow-capped mountain with the Judean hills. The angels might also have been apsaras, Buddhist floating spirits. That merging of Christ and Buddha held the promise of one-world unity, the belief that Jerry and I had cherished since that first glow of international folk songs at the fountain. In that moment I knew that I would find Jerry's essence in my life again, though not necessarily in Jerry's way.

Days later, on the beach near our country house, I walked in what I felt must surely be his bare footprints, remembering how he galloped along the sand before diving into a wave. I didn't come there for solace, although the shore, with its endlessness of sky and sea, its absence of boundaries, did soften my thoughts about life's brevity. Back indoors, I played a CD of Tino Rossi singing "J'Attendrai," in honor of Bastille Day, which fell two weeks after he died. Again, I followed my own rituals. The more traditional customs would not serve, since no marriage had been like ours.

Neither would a service have consoled me. Jerry was a committed scientist, an unbeliever. I wanted to pray without the interference of a rabbi neither of us knew. We had opted for cremation, and at the Plaza Jewish Community Chapel I signed a sheaf of papers, wincing when the agent notified me they would have to remove Jerry's defibrillator.

Both of us together, each apart. They came back to me, the rabbi's spoken words at our wedding ceremony. However close the union, you live apart, alone. Your freedom of choice, terrible in its way, is existentially important. As Whitman knew, nobody else can travel that road for you. And now you die alone. In our wills we had asked to have our ashes scattered in places we loved: Gerard Park and Louse Point in East Hampton, Washington Square in New York. In our country backyard, in the shade of that American beech tree whose leaves turn silver in winter but never fall, I dug a deep hole and filled it with most of the ashes, covering the mound with a stone circle. I remembered how, in our drive through southwest England, he'd stopped the car to stand silent before an oval bank said to be a Neolithic remnant. "Just think of how many wars have passed over these stones," he remarked.

My friends Philip Schultz and his wife, Monica Banks, poet and sculptor, respectively, joined me in a little "service" around the tree. Phil read his poem "The Magic Kingdom," a favorite of mine:

> Bless this ice-glazed garden of bleached stones
> strewn like tiny pieces of moonlight
> in sand puddles,
> the wind's grievous sigh,

the singing light,
the salt, the salt!

I spoke a few lines of Psalm 15, which extols a man who is good, one who:

Walketh uprightly, and worketh righteousness,
and speaketh the truth in his heart.

Then we poured more of the ashes into the bay at Louse Point. Monica spoke of the white cloud she saw form in the water, astonished to find in it the same pattern as in the sky's cloud above us. A bird that Jerry had taught me to call a skimmer circled the bay, arrowed past us, then did a U-turn and, wing-flapping, steered toward the sky. I marveled at such long curves of flight in so short a life, and thought of our lives, hardly short but overflowing with past adventures and future plans.

And on the following day, Elise Paschen, a poet friend, came from Chicago to recite "The Windhover," with its kestrel hawk, as we poured the remaining ashes into Fireplace Bay. A tern called, flying toward us, in a fitting elegy for the watcher of shorebirds.

Alone, I reread the Psalms, though I could not believe in them. Praise God who made my husband suffer so? Skeptical at first, I lingered on Psalm 90, whose lines emphasize the brevity of life, and adjure us to celebrate all else in the world, all we know and have:

So teach us to number our days, that we may
apply our hearts to wisdom.

During Jerry's sickness and in response to 90, I wrote "Poem Ending with a Phrase from the Psalms":

> Here where loss spins the hickory's dry leaves,
> rolls miles under wheels, and bleaches reeds
> that shone wine-red, I invoke a rose
> still rising like a choir, past its prime
> on a spindly bush that bore scarce blooms,
> as I wake to hear a jay screech like a gate
> swung open, and see your hand enfolding mine
> on linen: teach us to number our days.

Now the Kaddish rings in my head, an Aramaic prayer often said at Jewish funerals. Although it hallows the dead, it has in it not a word about death.

A line by Hopkins comes to me, "I wretch lay wrestling with (my God!) my God." I remember Jerry's sudden, conflicted evocation of God in the days before his death. And with it, resounding plangent, is Jacob's cry to the angel he wrestles, "I will not let thee go except thou bless me." Jerry would never have let go, but death overcame his tenacity.

For me there is no letting go. Details call for attention. His wishes will have to be carried out. In the fall I'll go to the concerts on the tickets Jerry ordered knowing he probably wouldn't live until then. Seven pairs of them attest to the power of his wish to live. Until then, resolved to do everyday tasks, I'll go through a normal morning when suddenly grief arrives in a high whitecap wave: after another lull, the comber rises and flattens me. Still, I find in the breaker's aftermath a place for the work that clarifies. Into the northeaster at sea a dinghy comes, splintered, in need of repair. I climb aboard and try to bail it out. I go on.

"They say time heals grief; it doesn't; it emphasizes it." So wrote Marianne Moore, and it's true. In the months following Jerry's death, the pain of reality replaced the initial shock.

My walks through city and country were not cures but bandages. In the city I wandered miles uptown from Washington Square Park to the Conservatory Garden, now past its spring bloom, where we had sat under crabapple blossoms, wandered through pale yellow narcissi, and had looked over the tulip beds. Our sojourns had happened a decade before, but even then we thought of mortality, wondering for an instant whether we would be alive when the spirea bloomed in fall.

In the apartment, his things would stay. Objects are a part of us; we look at things and see ourselves. Jerry's clothes stayed in the closet along with his walkers, weights, massagers, and stretch bands. I imagined him in his midnight-blue blazer and pearl-gray wool slacks, his paler blue turtleneck that accented his darting hazel eyes and showed off his fair skin. I pictured him in the shoes he wore to concerts, the shiny cordovan lace-ups he placed on the footrest of his wheelchair when he could no longer walk.

I resubscribed to his *Scientific American* and *Nature*, intending to learn all I could of his science research. I reordered his *Physicians' Desk Reference*. His blood-pressure cuff and his blue pencil box, containing those dutifully sharpened yellow No. 2 pencils, lay on the motorized chair.

In those early days, too unstrung to phone, I sent e-mails to friends, composing them individually, such as,

*My beloved husband, Jerome, died at home on
June 30 of cardiac failure. I had the honor of caring
for him in those last months.*

A letter came to me from Alfred Corn, a devoted Christian
with an uncanny knowledge of Jewish ritual:

*I have been thinking of you and Jerry today. This
evening, after the lighting of candles, and a reading of
Kaddish, I moved the mind to him and thought back
over the past three decades. He was a man large in
stature, a man of few words, a man of science and
reason. Consider the possibility that he fought hard
to stay here because he worried that you would not
flourish without his support. But the fact is, you will.
For one thing, though the body is gone, his essence
remains. That is still there within you, available as a
constant resource. You will even find that the relationship continues to deepen and to evolve. The dross will
wash away, leaving only the pure spirit, gentler and
more understanding.*

*"Love is as strong as death." So says the Song of
Songs; and I would not be the person to question it.
Perhaps that is why we are able to say the Kaddish:
"Yitgadal v'yitkadash sh'mei raba b'alma di-v'ra
chirutei, v'yamlich malchutei b'chayeichon."*

*"Glorified and sanctified be God's great name
throughout the world which He has created according
to His will. . . . He who creates peace in His celestial
heights, may He create peace for us and for all Israel;
and say, Amen."*

There is consolation in the future, Grace, good times,
love, laughter. And peace. Alfred.

I did not find peace. But Alfred's words were lifting. As
was the wisdom of Carol Muske-Dukes, when I had told her
about the waves of grief enfolding me as I watched shorebirds
at the bay.

I could hear her voice as I read:

Alas, I know about those "waves"—and how
they up-end you, spin you in the breaker-line—just
when you thought you might be getting back on your
feet, standing upright. But they do recede, don't
they? And then there are the skimmers and terns and
the real bay and the music.

I'm not sure that wished-for things are ever
believable—that "love is as strong as death." But we
must believe something is unceasing, in order to go on
with our lives. I will never celebrate death—it is cru-
el and indiscriminate—it crushes children and youth
and cripples and annihilates the old. Yet it cannot
entirely erase us. And I know that our relationships
with the dead go on—and on. Perhaps they deepen—
certainly they are filled with new pained wonder in
the altered presences of the lost.

And a letter came from William and Paula Merwin in
Hawaii, Paula's handwriting telling me that William's vision
was failing him:

The news came as a shock, although we knew
he'd been in poor health for some time, because he

was so much a part of your life, and always there in
our minds whenever we thought of you. I remember
when William and I were first together, you and
he were among the very first of his friends that I
met. What a gentle, quiet, kind man he has always
seemed to me—and devoted to you . . .

When I started teaching classes in the fall of 2016, two
months after Jerry's death, I had, besides a broken heart, a
broken foot. Three weeks earlier, hoping for distraction from
the pain of grief, I hiked the long peninsula of Gerard Park in
East Hampton. I was watching shorebirds, an osprey's high
flight on wide, serrated wings, an American oystercatcher's red
beak. Gazing upward, failing to notice what was in my path,
I fell on rocks that had been piled up for the making of a sea
wall. Pain raged, but fortunately not in my driving foot, and I
drove to a clinic for an X-ray. And, yes, I had a stress fracture
and was given a boot cast for six weeks. A hard sentence. In
the city, though limping, I was relieved to begin classes.

My students were absorbing, especially the ones whose
eyes lit up across centuries when they responded to a poem
by John Donne. I delighted in even routine tasks, such as
preparing roll books and calendars. But coming home nights
was another matter. Regrets poured out with the brandy in
my snifter glass. Why hadn't I stayed with Jerry every minute
of that last day, instead of ducking down to the park for ice
cream? I went over in my mind how he sank into the capacious
recliner by my desk, his eyes wide, his jaw relaxed, his speech
coming clearly only to say my name and declare his love. I
was thankful that he recognized me, unlike the home health

worker he'd taken for an Army technician he'd known in 1954. I attributed the confusion to his cardiac failure, causing an insufficient flow of oxygen to his brain. Still, his unlikeness to himself spurred me to run out for that cherry-vanilla cone.

I could have waited, perhaps forestalling his collapse. I could have complimented him, weeks earlier, on his Harris-tweed jacket, made in Donegal, that I found in his closet, and on the striped lavender shirt he wore. I could even have urged him to adopt children with me and raised the family he wanted. "I could haves" taunted me. And why couldn't I cry? Other than the night of the disconnect, other than shouts of rage to the shorebirds in Long Island, I was impassive.

Then one day my former student, Pooka Paik, brought cookies he'd baked following a recipe from his native Seoul, in Korea. His family was now in America. At Baruch he'd been graduated with honors, earning a Bachelor of Arts in English.

Pooka told me that his father had discouraged expressions of sadness, joy, and even pride. Early in Pooka's life, his best friend had been stabbed to death, and he broke the family taboo to cry aloud at his loss. His father had roundly punished him for it, and there began a series of violent lashings out, fortunately none of them incurring physical harm, though they delayed his college career. When he finally arrived at Baruch at age twenty-two, he took Great Works and read the *Iliad*.

The epic changed him utterly. Achilles's wrath became Pooka's. He read of Achilles's raw fury in war and his final recognition that violence must be curbed to uphold human values. He savored Achilles's wish that "strife could die from the lives of gods and men." But when Patroclus, Achilles's beloved friend, died in battle and Achilles lay fallen, "letting loose a terrible, wrenching cry," Pooka was renewed. He continued to live at home, but he refused to accept his family's repressive dicta. What's more, he would major in English literature, gobbling up the classics, though such a commitment had never before been considered in Pooka's household.

Pooka's story resounded in my mind. As a writer I knew solitude, but none like this one, filled with anguish. As Pooka had traveled Achilles's path in battle, I decided I would find my way through a dark wood of my imagining. I would struggle through that forest, bruised on thorns, in the frail, persistent hope of a bright clearing.

I arranged a memorial, or rather a celebration of Jerry's life, on October 24. It was well attended, for I had written to everyone I could think of who knew him, however slightly. Photos were flashed on a screen, Mozart's *Ave Verum* played over a speaker. Jerry would have approved of the multicultural audience composed of artists, writers, and scientists from many countries. My Baruch undergraduates attended, looking their best in suits and dress sweaters I'd not seen them wear before. There, too, were the older students from the Y classes I taught.

Dr. Thomas Moran, Jerry's colleague at Mount Sinai, spoke of Jerry as a scientist, educator, and mentor. To the interdisciplinary listeners, he gave details about the global adoption of Jerry's virus research; his experiments had spurred the development of vaccines and drugs. He said that Jerry's studies "documented the kinetics of the human responses to flu." With a team of scientists, he and Jerry had examined responses critical to recovery from virus infection.* Together with Dr. Peter

---

*Carolina B. Lopez, Thomas M. Moran, Jerome L. Schulman, and Ana Fernandez-Sesma, "Antiviral Immunity and the Role of Dendritic Cells," *International Journal of Immunology* 21, 339-353.

Palese, they mapped the genome of the influenza virus, developing something called the headless vaccine, which became the origin of the universal vaccine in progress now.

Dr. Moran's talk was yet another revelation. For years I had thought Jerry had refrained from talking about the technical side of his work because of my gaps of knowledge. Now, hearing Dr. Moran speak to that interdisciplinary audience, I saw Jerry anew. In my mind he stood there charmingly self-effacing, drawing friends out, finding it easier to recommend to a friend, or even a colleague, a new recording of Rutter's Requiem, than to talk about his findings of animal models for influenza A and B viruses. In that moment I knew the meaning of the adage I had rejected, "He will be with you." I believed it now, having learned more about him, and knew I'd continue to do so.

Monica Yates Shapiro and Sharon Yates Levine, Dick's lovely daughters, spoke of Jerry's impact on them as children. Monica, who had visited during his last week, told of seeing "that strong, steady, amusing man twinkling out his last days with humor." Though Monica is married and a mother of four, I've thought of her always as a child I had to shield from the dips in our marriage. To my proud surprise, she acknowledged them by saying, "A love story is what you had. He was worthy of every question you ever asked yourself about him and every yes you ever gave him. He was a hero."

CODA

He first deceased her; she for a little tried
To live without him, liked it not, and died.

Sir Henry Wotton (1568–1639)

Six months since Jerry died. Grief still arrives in high waves, but so does joy. Time emphasizes both. One luminous wave flows in when I go alone to the Philharmonic on opening night, on the tickets Jerry had bought. I keep his seat vacant. On the program is Dvořák's "New World" Symphony, and I thrill to the English horn, remembering that we heard it before, just after the tragedy of 9/11.

On these shorter, winter days I'm elated by the afternoon sun that streams through an enormous, transparent ceiling at the Met Museum and bares the legs of Greek and Roman sculptures. By a line by Paul Celan—"there is ever the sea, fire-red"—or by a page from Nabokov's *Speak, Memory*. By the balcony of a Stanford White building overlooking Forty-Third Street. By Alfred Brendel or Vladimir Feltsman playing Schubert's Impromptu in G-flat Major. By John Coltrane's tenor sax in *Kind of Blue*, or by Vivaldi's Gloria on a disc remastered from a long-playing record Jerry and I bought days after we met. By a TCM rerun of *La Strada* or by Nancy LaMott singing "On My Way to You" on the Jonathan Schwartz radio hour. By Arnold Schoenberg's *A Survivor from Warsaw*, a Holocaust cantata performed with Beethoven's upbeat Ninth Symphony, with its "Ode to Joy," at Lincoln Center. By a Poetry Revel at Baruch College, where eager students try out their newest work and listen to others. By the inviting face of a young neighbor, already an old friend. I wish Jerry were with me. And he is. In our long marriage there came an hour when we crossed a line and won the clear title to each other's joys, angers, and pains. I live in them now.

Acknowledgments

For scientific background and information I wish to thank Dr. Peter Palese and Dr. Thomas Moran of the Mount Sinai Department of Virology. I'm also grateful to Dr. Rhonda Rosenberg, a scientist who helped me assemble Dr. Schulman's papers, and who wrote to me her belief that his work "not only paved the way to neuraminidase inhibitors but also foreshadowed their limits."

For their help and kindness I'm grateful to Michael Blumenthal, Mary Ann Caws, Jennifer Clement, Alfred Corn, Dr. Antonio Gomes, Gail Levin, Elizabeth Macklin, Carol Muske-Dukes, Caroline Price, Dr. Carol Shoshkes Reiss, Philip Schultz, Susan Shapiro, Brian Swann, Benjamin Taylor, and Deanne Urmy. Thanks to Jonathan Rabinowitz, who asked me one day, unwittingly, if I'd ever written a memoir, and to Ruth Greenstein, my inspiring editor. And to Jerry, always and always.

For their compassion and support I thank my students, Susan McQuillan, Miguel Machado, Sarah Park, Andrew "Pooka" Paik, Benjamin Long, Kyah Saw Htoon, and Genesis Valdes.